GROWING UP IN AMERICA SERIES

BARTHOLD FLES, *Editor*

BIG CITY,
LITTLE BOY

By MANUEL KOMROFF

Coronet

A New York Tempest

Feast of the Jesters

Two Thieves

Jesus Through the Centuries

All in Our Day

I, the Tiger

Waterloo

March of the Hundred

Echo of Evil

The Travels of Marco Polo (Editor)

Jade Star

BIG CITY,
LITTLE BOY

By

MANUEL KOMROFF

A. A. WYN, INC., NEW YORK

CONTENTS

◇◇◇◇◇◇◇◇◇◇◇◇◇◇◇◇◇◇◇◇◇◇◇◇◇◇◇◇◇◇

		Page
ONE	THE ENCHANTED ISLE	3
TWO	THE NEW CENTURY	73
THREE	SPRING AND SUMMER	99
FOUR	LADY LIBERTY	125
FIVE	A BUSHEL OF EXPERIENCE	149

1

The Enchanted Isle

*T*HE VERY BEST PLACE FOR A BOY to be born is on an enchanted isle. And that is just where I was born—in New York City, on the enchanted island of Manhattan.

New York was a wonderful place. It was a city of granite-block streets, brownstone houses, lace curtains, rubber plants, and spittoons. It was a city of saloons, orphanages, poverty in hovels, great wealth in mansions. There were horse-drawn streetcars and stagecoaches on Fifth Avenue. There were coachmen in high boots with long whips, street vendors with singsong cries, and hokeypokey men. There were children at labor, women in feather boas and high button shoes, and men with beards. There were rattling steam trains that brought in the cattle from the West, and there were sailing schooners whose great bowsprits jutted out overhead halfway across the river-front streets. The time was just before the turn of the century in the 1890's.

This was a time that had grown tired of being old and was getting ready to become a new time. It was a time of great change. Life, manners, and thought were being re-molded. The grip of Victorianism was being broken.

The world that my eyes first saw was a world teeming

with life. All the races of man were to be found on the streets of New York. Here, side by side in peace, lived Europeans, Orientals, Negroes, Red Men, and Gypsies. And out of this mixture came Americans.

As there was variety in races and nationalities, so there was also variety in occupations. Those who lived on Manhattan brought with them from their distant homelands all sorts of trades and skills. Besides the ordinary butchers, bakers, and candlestick makers, one found rug-weavers from Turkey, highly skilled cabinetmakers from China and Japan, diamond-cutters from Holland, lacemakers from France and Belgium, and Spanish cigar makers—an endless list of unusual occupations. Here on Manhattan was a miniature world.

This was the world into which I was born. And from the very start I loved it. As far back as I can remember I felt that I belonged to the city and that the city belonged to me. And since the city belonged to me, I felt free to wander about anywhere I chose, observing and inspecting everything. When I was very young I naturally could not wander too far afield, but it was not very long before I grew older and bolder, and in time I explored every section of New York.

In spite of being warned of the danger of being shanghaied—and in those days many boys were carried off to sea —I spent long hours wandering along the water-front. Here I loved to walk under the bowsprits of the schooners and look up through a maze of ropes and rigging to the blue sky. When a good ocean-going schooner, a four- or five-master, was tied up beside a dock its forward rigging almost touched the old buildings of the street. And it was wonderful to see the neatly bundled sails that were tied to the masts with millions of ropes.

But not all the boats that docked in the rivers around the island were schooners. There were great iron ocean-going steamers, yachts, ferryboats, tugboats, and barges. And each had its own life and fascination.

The ocean-going vessels came from distant ports. Some came from Europe, others from South America, China, Japan, Africa, and Australia. They all came here to my enchanted island, bringing strange cargoes and strange crews. On the river-front streets one saw many Malay, Chinese, and African Negro sailors dressed in their colorful native costumes.

But ships from foreign ports were only one of the wonders that I knew. Down the long center of Manhattan Island to Forty-second Street stretched four railroad tracks over which rolled great steam trains bringing passengers, mail, and freight from the Wild West and from cities as far off as San Francisco on the Pacific coast.

To stand on the bank of the open railway cut on Park Avenue and see the thundering and rattling trains come in was a hypnotic sight for any boy. Watching the old horses in the train yard turn the engines on a revolving platform could occupy many hours. And I was not the only boy to stand and watch. There was always plenty of company. The steam, smoke, sizzling pistons, and great driving-wheels held us spellbound. It did not matter to us that Park Avenue was lined with noisy factories, sordid tenements with backyard privies, and wooden hovels, all caked with black soot. To us, standing there watching the wonderful trains, Park Avenue was heaven.

But I did not spend all my time watching boats and trains. There were other things that I had to inspect. I wandered downtown through the different foreign districts—through Little Italy, Chinatown, the Ghetto, and streets where Turks and Syrians smoked hookah pipes. In other parts of the city I wandered through Hungarian, French, Negro, German, and Spanish districts. I heard strange languages and saw people dressed in what remained of their native costumes. I peered into grocery stores and saw all kinds of foods I had never seen before.

And far down at the end of the Island in the oldest part of the city, where there still stood beautiful Colonial homes that dated back to before the American Revolution, before George Washington was inaugurated on Wall Street, I roamed through streets taken over by wholesalers. There was one street where nothing but coffee was sold, another for cheese, one for rope and hemp, one for cotton bales, and one for oil and olives. There were still others where other produce was sold. A boy with a keen nose could tell at any moment where he was!

Then, too, I visited the great open markets to which each day the farmers brought their vegetables and the fishermen their fish. I saw cattle being driven down First Avenue to the slaughterhouses. And up on Twenty-fourth Street there was a special market that occupied a great deal of my time. This was the horse market.

Several times each week crowds would gather here on the open street to attend the horse auctions. All kinds of horses came to the block. Some were carriage horses with proud manes and prancing gaits, and some were fine saddle horses, but most were wagon and truck horses. And many of them were underfed and showed marks of abuse. Occasionally some Irish hunters would be sold, and it even happened that Arabian steeds came up for auction.

All the horses to be sold were trotted up and down the street by stable boys smartly dressed as jockeys. This was done to exhibit the animals to the buyers. And as they were led back and forth the bystanders argued the horses' points among themselves and cracked their whips to liven up the horses' gaits. It was easy for a boy to learn a lot about horses just by watching and listening.

Several blocks, running eastward on Twenty-fourth Street, were lined with stables, blacksmith shops, and stores where saddles and harnesses were made and sold. Here boxes of whips stood at the doorways—fine varnished whips for carriages and crude whips for wagons. In these stores were sold boots, spurs, bits, bridles, feed bags, horse blankets, blocks of salt, and all kinds of other necessities. Here also were sold rosettes and other decorations for harnesses and special comforts for the horse, such as straw hats for the summer sun and string net coverings to keep the flies away. The best of these stores always had, outside on the sidewalk, life-size wooden horses beautifully painted, with shiny brown glass eyes. I thought them very beautiful and should have liked to own one.

There was still another place on Manhattan that demanded a good bit of my attention. This was Central Park. Here in the summer one could go boating on a beautiful lake or roam over acres of green grass as soft and smooth as a carpet. Here, too, in the winter one went ice-skating and sleigh-riding.

But the most wonderful thing about Central Park was the zoo with its lions and tigers, its elephants and hippopotamuses, its camels and buffaloes, its bears and wolves, and its wonderful house filled to the brim with monkeys!

No matter where one went in New York, there were interesting things. The city was teeming with life. The streets were filled with people, bicycles, pushcarts, wagons; with private carriages, horse-drawn buses, and hackney coaches. And everywhere one went there were street cleaners busy sweeping up the horse manure. They worked very hard, for there were lots of horses. And at each corner the street-cleaners made hills of manure, which were later carted away in wagons. These piles of manure gave a horsy flavor to the air —a healthy smell, aromatic and spicy. They also provided feeding grounds for thousands of fat insolent sparrows filled with noisy chatter. And this manure had still another use. It often happened that as a drunk came staggering out of one of the many city saloons the young street blades would push him into a pile just for the sport of the thing!

And besides interesting sights and things, the city was filled with excitement. One could always count on a runaway horse, a robbery, a street fight, or a good blazing fire. And it was a thrilling sight to see the fire engines, drawn by great spirited horses, race over the granite-block streets with sparks flying from the horses' iron shoes as well as from the engine's nickel-plated boiler. The steam whistles blew, the bells clanged, and all the boys for blocks around followed on the run. A good blazing fire with people scrambling down ladders or jumping into nets was truly a sight to see.

Yes, there is no question about it, I was born on an enchanted island.

To add to my good fortune my grandfather owned a cigar store on Third Avenue and Fifty-second Street. My grandparents and I lived in an apartment above the store. To me this place was the crossroads of the world, for it was ideally situated. It was around the corner from a firehouse and a police station. It was not far from the railroad tracks on Park Avenue and only two blocks away from my school. Everything was handy. Besides, it was in the heart of the Irish district, where there were lots of saloons with crossed shillelaghs in the windows and Gaelic was freely spoken. To live among the Irish is always lively.

Into this store each day came all kinds of people. And from as far back as I can remember I was there helping Grandpa and listening to all that was said.

A good part of our trade came from policemen, in blue uniforms with a row of large brass buttons down the center and high bowler hats, There were also detectives and firemen. They came to buy cigars, chewing tobacco, and snuff, and they brought with them the news of the day. They told Grandpa about all their bold adventures. One day they raided a gambling house. Another time they captured a gang of counterfeiters; and they showed us some of the fake money. The firemen, too, had stories to relate—stories of brave rescues and narrow escapes. They told harrowing tales of children trapped in burning tenements and stories of horses being rescued from flaming stables.

Besides firemen, detectives, and policemen, Grandpa had many other customers. And there were some who came almost every day. Mrs. O'Leary was always running short of snuff; Adolph Schultz, the fiddle-maker from around the corner, always needed more cigars; Mr. Hadley came for pipe tobacco; and Mr. Quaff, an actor from the actors' boarding-house on Lexington Avenue, smoked many Pittsburgh stogies, two for a nickel.

Mrs. O'Leary was cheerful and friendly. Her pale blue eyes had a lively twinkle and her tongue a salty tang. She complained only of her rheumatism, but it did not keep her from attending early morning mass every day in the year. Summer and winter she wore a gray plaid shawl over her drab black dress. She used large quantities of Copenhagen snuff, which she inhaled with great pleasure. An ounce lasted her only about two days; then she was back for more.

Schultz, the fiddle-maker, had many opinions. He was against science, against machinery, against change, against progress. Since fiddles could not be improved, neither could the world. He believed that Bismarck was the greatest man the world had ever known and that the Kaiser was his natural heir.

Mr. Hadley was just the opposite. He was always dreaming of the future, and he was in favor of change. He had his own private views of everything. Popular opinion meant nothing to him. He was irritating, and his liberal views irritated my grandfather; yet I often heard Grandpa admit, and with respect, that Mr. Hadley had an independent mind.

Mr. Quaff had once been a Shakespearean actor in Booth's company. Later he specialized in church readings and recitations. He was always "in rehearsal" but never on the stage. And yet he was always on the stage, for every movement he made, every word he uttered was studied and dramatic. He lived in a world of plays, acting, books, and painting. He was different and he was interesting. One day he declaimed lines from Hamlet and another day he would recite for you passages from Henry Irving's popular melodrama, *The Bells*. All this appealed to me.

These were but a few of the vast gallery of people who came regularly to our cigar store.

Guarding the entrance to the store was a serious-faced wooden Indian. He stood on the sidewalk at one side of the door, and in his outstretched hand he held a bundle of cigars. He wore a headdress of carved feathers bound to his bronzed brow with a tight gold band. His costume was gaily painted in clear primitive colors.

And every spring Grandpa gave him a fresh coat of paint, varnish, and gold leaf. For many years I served as a willing assistant, until I was old enough to undertake the responsibility of repainting the Indian all by myself.

Now, painting a wooden Indian is not so easy a task as one might think. First one has to be sure of the weather. Then there are different-colored paints to be mixed and serious decisions to be made about changes in the color scheme. One year our Indian's buckskin shirt was yellow and his skirt bright red, another year they were green and orange. It all depended on how we felt at the time and what paint was at hand. The feather headdress was easy. Each feather took a bright color of its own. But no matter how many

varied costumes our Indian wore through the years, his skin
and his cigars remained the same dark brown.

While the wooden Indian guarded the door the inside of
Grandpa's cigar store was ruled over by a Negro boy made
of metal. He stood proudly on a slab of white marble before
a long mirror. In his mouth he had a cigarette from which
burned a small gas jet ever ready to light cigars and cigarettes. On either side of this happy Negro boy were two jars,
one containing splints that you could light at the gas flame,
the other filled with sand in which to extinguish the flaming
splint.

Opposite the Negro boy on his marble slab were a long
counter and showcases filled with boxes of cigars. Behind
this on a shelf stood six or seven large snuff jars containing
brands imported from Holland, Denmark, and Ireland.
Brass scales with a set of weights stood on the counter. And
close at hand were horn spoons for ladling the moist snuff
into small glazed paper bags.

Grandfather also carried a varied line of pipe tobacco,
stogies, and cut plug for chewing. Close to the brass scales,
on top of the counter, there stood a large cutter for slicing
the plug tobacco. Chewing tobacco was very popular, and
Grandpa sold a great deal in five- and ten-cent slices. In
fact, everything in the place sold for either five or ten cents.
I don't mean to say that Grandpa did not have one or two
good customers. He did. There was Dr. Lambert for in-
stance, from fashionable Lexington Avenue, where people
had crossed swords on the wall and Turkish dens. He bought
his cigars by the box. Each box cost him two dollars and

fifty cents. And I was always called into service to deliver his order.

There was another item that Grandpa handled: cigarettes. But cigarettes and those who smoked them were frowned upon. There was something wicked about this form of tobacco.

"Loafers!" Grandpa always said. "Only loafers smoke cigarettes."

And I knew by the tone of his voice that all cigarette smokers would come to a bad end.

But the cigarette manufacturers were not going to be put off by prejudice. They printed gay posters which they tacked up in all tobacco stores. And some of them even resorted to including pictures of popular actresses, dressed in tights, inside each package of cigarettes. Young men collected these pictures and carried them about in their pockets. And when they had duplicates they exchanged with each other. Little by little, year by year, more and more cigarettes were sold. And in the end snuff and chewing tobacco lost out, and cigarettes became very popular. Even women began to smoke them. But for some reason the use of cigarettes was considered immoral, and public opinion was against it. A lady was arrested in Central Park and charged with disorderly conduct for smoking a cigarette while riding in her open carriage.

To supplement the earnings of his cigar store Grandpa also ran another business: he accepted classified advertisements for the daily newspapers. This separate affair was conducted on the top of an old desk at the rear of the store. It was a simple business requiring only a small overhead, some torn sheets of writing paper, a few pens and blotters, and a bottle of ink.

It was a simple business, but it brought a great deal of excitement into our lives. Through this advertising agency my grandfather and I knew everything that happened in the neighborhood. We were the first to know if a man were looking for a new job, if someone needed a servant or had a piano for sale. We were the first to hear of a missing heir, or a lost dog, or a stolen horse. And for lost-and-found advertisements my grandfather always recommended the phrase "No questions asked."

Some of the people wrote out their own advertisements, but many asked Grandpa to help them. He was very good at helping; he knew all the special phrases and how to save a word or two. He wrote the advertisements in a clear hand with a needle-sharp pen point. But he always had difficulty with his pen, which picked up fluff from the paper and sludge from the bottom of the inkwell. When this happened he would quickly wipe the pen on the side of his head. By the end of the week the right side of his white head was inky black. Grandma and I could always tell the state of the business by the amount of ink on Grandpa's head.

Yes, people came to us with all kinds of problems. And Grandpa and I knew almost everything that went on in the neighborhood.

How often have I seen a harried man come into the store and, pointing at my grandfather, say: "I am no longer responsible for my wife's debts. She has left my bed and board. Write out a personal and keep it within two lines. She's not worth more expense!"

How often have I seen a widow, or deserted wife, advertising for a lost son or a missing husband! And with such advertisements we heard whole chapters of troubled lives, sagas of sorrow.

I listened to every word that was said, and I learned a great many things. The cigar store was a university of life, an academy of manners. And I sucked it all up like a sponge. Here, without tortuous books or troublesome teachers, I was educated without pain.

At eight o'clock each night, when all the advertisements were in their proper envelopes together with the correct amount of money, Grandpa and I would put on our hats and coats and, leaving Grandma in charge of the store, start out for Newspaper Row.

It was an easy trip. Grandpa and I walked north along Third Avenue for only one block. Here we climbed two long flights of stairs to the elevated station above. Grandpa was always puffing hard when he got to the top, but it did not bother me at all; in fact, I took the steps two at a time. I was always eager for a ride on the elevated steam train.

I always waited for Grandpa at the top of the steps, because he had to buy the ticket. We needed only one ticket for both of us, for in those days children under seven rode free. Later on, of course, as I grew taller and could no longer pass for seven, Grandpa had to buy two tickets. At any rate, during the early days Grandpa bought only one five-cent ticket at the booth. This he would hand to me, for I had the privilege of dropping it into the ticket box under the stern gaze of the ticket chopper. Once past the box we were on the platform, and I quickly surveyed the track to see if our train were approaching. On some days we were lucky and the train was close by.

The small steam engine that pulled the rattling cars had a highly polished copper boiler and lots of brass pipes. It was run by an engineer who also served as fireman. Often while the train was stopped at some station and the passengers were getting off and on, the engineer would hurry over to a coal bin at the front end of the platform for a shovelful or two of coal. This he would throw into the flaming firebox. Then, with a sharp toot on the steam whistle, he would start the train, and after a dozen heavy puffs the engine would gather momentum and we would be on our way. The entire trip from the cigar store to the newspaper world on Park Row took only about half an hour. But that half hour was filled with all kinds of interest.

To begin with, as the train traveled downtown and stopped at the different stations, almost every station marked a different national district. At Fifty-third Street the Irish got on, at Fourteenth Street there were Germans, at Eighth Street Hungarians, at Grand Street Jews, and at Chatham Square Chinese and Italians. Sitting there on the train we joined with the races of man and we heard smatterings of many foreign tongues. And as the train passed between the stations high above the streets one could peer through endless windows into the privacy of the houses along the way. Each window opened into a home. And everywhere there were dismal green-walled kitchens, restless children, men asleep in tousled beds, dusty rubber plants, and fat women leaning out of windows. It was all a little raw, but it was life.

At length, when we reached Brooklyn Bridge station, Grandpa and I would get off the train and hurry over to the newspaper buildings, which were all near by. Here was the hub of all news. In those days newspapers were the main source of information on world and local events. Everyone read the papers; and there were a great many different papers published. Newspapers were a nerve center of city life. And Grandpa and I felt privileged to have entrée into this important world. Very often we learned important news hours before the rest of the city.

While my grandfather took care of his business I would wander about, in and out of the different newspaper rooms, watching everything that was going on. Here was a world all its own. And I liked it.

It did not make any difference what room I wandered into, there was always something exciting going on. In one room filled with cigar smoke, men wearing green eyeshades and in shirt sleeves sat at long tables working on copy. Some ran telegraph machines and typewriters. Others wrote the headlines with soft black pencils on sheets of newspaper stock. These words would become what I called the big words. I was much impressed with the big-word writers. The rest of the men wrote little words, ordinary newspaper words.

In other rooms the copy was cast into linotype slugs. These linotype rooms were always hot and filled with fumes that came from the many pots of molten type metal attached to the linotype machines. Operators sat at each machine typing the newspaper copy. These machines were wonderful to watch. The operator typed the words from his copy, and out came these very same words already cast in a line of metal type. It was all like magic.

In another room stereotypes of these same words were made into curved cylinders. Later these cylinders were sent downstairs and fitted into the giant presses, two stories high. These monsters of steel sucked in great rolls of paper, imprinted the paper with the words on the inked cylinders, and vomited out stacks of newspapers already cut, folded, counted, and ready for the newsboys.

No matter where I wandered on Newspaper Row, there was a pulse and throb to life, there was a rush and bustle unlike anything I knew. Even the air seemed different. It had a smell all its own—mingling of hot lead fumes, turpentine, paper, and cigar smoke. But in my childish mind it smelled of only one thing: electricity.

Uptown we used gas, and gas had its own smell. Therefore I felt that down here in the newspaper offices, where they had electric lights and telegraph machines, the air must be filled with the smell of electricity. In fact, I attributed the great activity in this newspaper world to the electricity they used in the offices. Electricity was a new thing, and one could imagine almost anything about it.

In time some of the men, seeing me wandering about night after night, became friendly. They even spoke to me. And when they did I had to answer them. This was not always easy for me, because I had a bad stammer.

"Hey, kid, where are you from, Brooklyn?"

I smiled, for I knew that this was a joke. How could anyone think I came from Brooklyn? "No, sir," I said. "I come from uptown."

"Where uptown?"

"Fifty-second Street."

"You get down here every night?"

"Yes, sir. My grandfather brings down your advertisements. He has an agency."

"How old are you?"

"Seven."

"You go to school?"

"Yes, sir, P.S. 18 on Fifty-first Street."

"Do you like school?"

"No, sir. I was left back last year."

"What do you learn in school?"

"All kinds of things—arithmetic, spelling, geography, and penmanship."

"Which do you like best?"

"Penmanship."

"Let me see you write your name. Here, take this pen."

I took the pen and wrote my name in a large bold hand.

"Pretty good," said the man, examining the script. "Now I know your name. Front name looks Spanish. Rear name Russian. Your people Spanish?"

I shook my head "No."

"Your people come from Russia?"

"Yes, sir."

"How long ago?"

"Don't know. My great-grandfather came over with my great-grandmother. And Grandpa came over too."

"Are your great-grandparents still alive?"

"My great-grandmother died. But my great-grandfather is alive."

"Where is he?"

"Sick in the hospital. Sometimes they take me to see him on Sundays."

"Must be pretty old man."

"Yes, sir. He's very old. Has a big white beard like Santa Claus, and he has a gold watch that you wind up with a key. The key is on his watch chain. And you know what? He's got a pistol, a real one. He has it in his satchel under his bed. Every time I see him I ask him about it, and sometimes he shows it to me. There are no bullets in it. He's very old. His hands shake."

"And your Grandpa brings you down here often?"

"Yes, sir, almost every night."

"He must like you?"

"Oh, yes, he does."

"You live with your grandparents?"

"Yes."

"Where are your own parents?"

"Divorced."

"Don't you ever see your mother?"

"See her all the time. Only she's busy."

"What doing?"

"She's a lawyer and works in the courts with the judges and everything."

"Is that so? Not many women lawyers in New York State."

"Nope. She's the second woman admitted to the bar."

"Must be smart."

"Yes, sir. Her picture was in the newspapers."

He looked at the slip of paper upon which I had written my name.

"I remember that name," he said. "She did have her picture in the papers. Was admitted to the bar only last year."

"Yes, sir," I repeated. "Her picture was in the papers."

"And where's your father?"

"He lives far away in some other state. He only comes to New York once in a while."

Now I saw my grandfather in the hall; his business was finished, and he was looking for me. And so I said a quick good-bye and ran to join him.

"What were you doing in there?" asked by grandfather.

"I was talking with that man."

"You know who he is?"

"No."

"Well, he's Mr. Stevens, one of the chief editors of this newspaper."

My grandfather was a good deal impressed that a man of Mr. Stevens's position should have bothered to talk with a seven-year-old boy, especially when that child was his grandson.

In the spring of that same year I had my first boat ride and my first visit to the country. My world was expanding. It all came about through the death of my great-grandfather.

The funeral procession consisted of a black horse-drawn hearse and three carriages. Grandpa, Grandma, and I rode in the first carriage. The other two carriages were filled with relatives. The procession drove slowly down Third Avenue, block after block, mile after mile. And Grandma cried all the way. But for me it was a nice excursion.

I sat beside the window and looked out. It was a beautiful spring day, and since everyone seemed to be out on the streets there were a lot of things going on. Women and men were standing about talking, children were playing games, and twice we passed dead horses in the street, waiting for the horse wagon to cart them away. We also passed some milestones on the edge of the sidewalks. They were all very old and weathered, but the number of miles to Boston could still be read.

The warm sunshine liberated the street odors; the smell of horse manure was blended with the odor of garbage and ash cans on the sidewalks. For me, sitting in the carriage, this was added to the smell of leather and horsehair. All together, I thought it a very good mixture.

We rode on and on, through the old Bowery and past City Hall. It was a long trip but a good one. At length we came to Bowling Green at the end of the island, and here the carriages stopped and waited in line for the Staten Island Ferry. We did not have to wait long; soon our carriages were on board, and the ferry pulled out of its slip.

Now I had seen many boats and ferries, but this was my first ride across water. And I wanted to get out of the carriage and inspect everything. Grandfather took me by the hand and led me around. We stuck our heads into the engine room and saw the pistons plunging up and down. We climbed to the upper deck and watched the great side-wheels churn the water as they went round and round. We saw the long white bubbling wakes. They looked like soda water to me. In the distance we could see the busy harbor shipping, and through the mist rose the great Statue of Liberty, guardian of the port.

I liked being on a boat, floating on the water with the wind blowing in my face. I liked the smell of the sea air. And I was sorry when we could see the Staten Island dock and we had to get back into our carriage.

Soon the ferry was bumping its way into its slip, and there was a groaning of the wooden piles and a rattling of chains. There was a lot of noise; then there was quiet, and the carriages started to roll off the boat, down the gangplank, on to the pier.

Now the funeral procession started on the road that led to the cemetery, at a place called Silver Lake. We rode slowly on over dirt roads with loose stones. We passed trees in groves and open fields in which stood cows and horses eating green grass instead of hay. We heard the clear notes of birds that were not sparrows.

Staten Island seemed a queer place to me. There weren't any sidewalks, the roads were not paved with granite blocks, and the houses were all wooden and very far apart. I did not understand it all, and I was surprised. Until then I had thought that the whole world was made up of other places just like New York City, with rows and rows of brownstone houses, long avenues and streets crowded with people, carriages and wagons. I had always thought that the trains and boats that came to my enchanted island connected one city with another. It had never occurred to me that there could be great stretches of country that looked like Central Park, only not so neatly kept. Suddenly my idea of the world was changed, and I did not feel very comfortable about it.

But after riding for another mile or so I thought to myself that maybe it was all right; maybe it was a good idea for some places to be cities and other places to be country.

In time our little procession reached Silver Lake Cemetery, and we all got out of the carriages and gathered around a great hole in the ground into which my great-grandfather's coffin was lowered. To me it looked like a deep black pit, and I did not like it. I thought it was not a nice thing to do to my great-grandfather. But Grandpa said that this was the way it always happened. When people died they had to be buried.

Two men started filling in the open grave. They shoveled the earth back into the pit. We all stood about, and everyone was very quiet. When the grave was finally filled there seemed to be a sudden release of tension. The one who was dead was now in his proper place. And the living were free and in the sunshine.

Slowly we now walked away from the grave. And here in this cemetery I found lots of things to do. There was tall grass to walk through, there were wild flowers to pick. And there was an old farmhouse where the caretaker lived. It was different from the houses I knew, and in the rear there were a grape arbor and an old well. I had never seen either before, and Grandpa had to tell me what they were. I liked the well the best.

I leaned against the wellhouse and looked down into a long black hole, and deep in the cool darkness I saw the shimmer of water. The bucket was attached to a windlass, and I could see how it worked. I turned the handle and watched it go down, down, down until it was almost lost in darkness. The rope slackened, and I knew it had hit the water. I held the handle tightly until the bucket filled; then I turned the handle again, raising the bucket heavy with water. When it reached the top there was the coldest, freshest water I had ever tasted. It was so good that I went about and offered tumblers of water to all my relatives. And I explained to them that this water came out of a hole in the ground, not out of a faucet at a sink. I offered them lots of water to drink, for I was anxious to send the bucket down on another trip. And between what they drank and what I spilled the bucket went down several times. It was good fun.

I was truly sorry when we had to climb back into our dusty carriages and start home. I thought that, in a way, it would be nice to stay out here on Staten Island. But when we were once more on the ferry and in the light of the setting sun I saw for the first time in my life the magical distant skyline of New York, I knew that this was where I wanted to be. This was my home. The country was very nice, but when it was dark I felt that I should be much safer in the city. And then, I reasoned, one could always visit the country; one did not really have to live there. It was more natural to live in a big city.

I spoke about this with Grandma and Grandpa as we rode back up Third Avenue, and they agreed with me. One could always visit the country.

After this each spring my grandmother and I went on a wonderful picnic. Once each year we went out to Staten Island to freshen up the graves. Of course, we didn't ride in

a private carriage. We took a horse-drawn streetcar down to
the Battery. Then we crossed over on the ferry, and from the
ferry-house to the cemetery we rode in a public coach. We
carried with us a basket of lunch: sandwiches, cake, fruit.
And we also carried some plants.

One year we planted a row of pansies, another year we
planted geraniums, and once we planted four small cedar
trees, one in each corner of the fenced-in-plot. It was a fair-
sized plot with only two graves, but Grandma explained:
"There is room here for eleven more."

On these yearly visits Grandma and I always worked very
hard. We dug in the fresh earth, set the plants in place, and
watered them thoroughly. When we were all through, it always looked very nice.

This was the only garden we ever had.

The first years of my life were spent during a time of
peace. The Civil War had ended some thirty years before,
and its wounds were pretty much healed. This bitter strife
had receded into the historical past, and everyone seemed to
believe that peace would now remain with us forever. There
was no reason to think otherwise.

But in 1898, when I was almost eight years old, something
suddenly happened many hundreds of miles away from
New York that changed our lives completely. It led to war;
and from that moment on there has never been a year of real
peace.

On a bleak winter's day, February 15, 1898, the U.S. Battleship *Maine* was mysteriously blown up in the harbor of
Havana, Cuba. The city first learned of this disaster, as it

learned of so many other things, from the newspapers. That afternoon the streets suddenly filled with newsboys crying: "Yextra, yextra! Read all about it!" Everyone bought a paper. There was not much news beyond the big words of the black headlines, but these were shaking. Everyone was stunned. Some enemy had dared destroy an American battleship. This certainly meant war. The word "war" was repeated over and over again.

Everyone who came into the cigar store agreed that things looked very bad.

"It smells like carnage to me," said Mrs. O'Leary, taking an extra large pinch of snuff. "But if a fight is what them Spaniards is looking for, they will have their hands full."

My Grandfather agreed. "A nation of seventy-five million people such as we have in the United States, with all our machinery and everything, can never be beaten."

And all the policemen and firemen agreed that this was a hotheaded act that would cost Spain plenty.

There was only one thing that I could not understand, and that was why everyone seemed worried at the possibility of war. This was strange. I thought it was about time we had a war. And I could see nothing but glory in the whole business. Having served an apprenticeship by running to fires and other disasters, I felt that I was ready for such a great adventure. In fact, quite early that afternoon I made up my mind that if war really came I would play a part in it.

That night my Grandfather and I left the cigar store earlier than usual. We were anxious to get down to the newspaper offices and learn the latest news.

When we reached Park Row everything seemed different.

Huge crowds stood before the bulletin board on the front of each newspaper building. And the streets were filled with wagons lined up ready to receive the special editions and race them to different parts of the city.

Inside the buildings all fury had broken loose. People ran through the halls shouting and waving papers and telegrams. The telegraph rooms were noisy and crowded, so that even an energetic boy who could wiggle like a fish had a hard time getting in. But I did manage to reach a redheaded fellow I knew by the name of Oscar.

"It's true?" I shouted in his ear.

"True, kid. The filthy swine blew up our battleship."

"Then it's war!"

"You can bet your life on that, kid. It's war! Nothing can stop it."

That was all I wanted to know. And if redheaded Oscar, who had his finger on the telegraph key, said it was war, then you could rest assured it would be war.

I got into the room where Mr. Stevens had his desk. But he did not notice me. A hundred mad people were running in and out, some in shirt sleeves and some in overcoats, some with green eyeshades and disheveled hair and some wearing their hats. A boy went from desk to desk with hot black coffee. The copy boys were on the run.

The biggest and blackest type ever used was splashed across the front pages. The extras came out hourly on the hour. Newsboys waited impatiently. And as soon as they got their bundles, as many papers as they could carry, they ran through the streets of my enchanted isle with the wild cry of "Yextra! Yextra! The *Maine!* War! Yextra! 250 dead! Yextra!" And in a few minutes their bundles of papers were gone and they were running back for more.

Grandpa and I wandered from one office to another. In one building I found a friend who, like redheaded Oscar, was a telegraph operator. I managed to get close to him and ask: "How about war? Not yet."

"No, kid. Not yet but soon."

I was disappointed.

Going home that evening on the elevated steam railway with my grandfather, I again asked: "No war yet, Grandpa, eh?"

"No, not yet. But it looks like a war with Spain," he said very sadly. "I'm afraid it can't be stopped. It's now up to the President and Congress. Maybe they can manage to avoid it. We'll just have to wait and see."

He seemed much depressed about this whole business, and I could not understand why. I did not say any more. But I was sure the telegraph men must be right. After all, they had their fingers right on the news. I just looked at Grandpa in silence, and secretly I thought how lucky I was. Not only did I live in the best place in the world, with fire engines and steam trains, but now we were going to have a war, a real war with Spain. And everybody was going to go and fight until the enemy was dead. Of course, not my grandfather. He couldn't go. He was too old. Besides, he had to take care of the old snuff jars and help the people compose their advertisements.

But I considered myself a person of just the proper experience for a war. I knew my way about the city streets. I knew how to avoid the street gangs and other loafers. My spelling was bad and I had a terrible stammer, but I could read and add and multiply big numbers. And I reasoned that a stammer would be lost in the noise of a big war. Besides, I could run like a streak, and in every army I was sure they needed messengers who were fast and smart. Then, too, I had read about drummer boys in the Civil War. If those boys could do it. . . . It couldn't be so hard to drum on a drum.

The next afternoon I was late in getting home from school. "Been marching," I announced proudly.

"Marching?" asked my grandfather.

"Yep. Marching in the school yard with the cadets. At first they wouldn't let me march with them. Said I was too young and too small. But I told them that I was taller than Tommy Schultz and Bobby Wilder. And they said I wasn't. And we measured up back to back and I was. I told them that in order of size I would stand number three in the line."

"Then they let you march?"

"No. They still wouldn't let me march. They said I had no uniform and I would spoil the looks of the whole company. I didn't answer, but when they started to march I marched along. I can do everything they can do. Right face, left face, about face, forward march, halt. It's easy."

"But you are too young," said my grandmother.

"Too young," added my grandfather.

How could anyone be too young for a war? I drew a slip of paper from my pocket. "Here is the place," I said, "where the boys get their uniforms. It is Browning, King & Company, on Cooper Square."

My grandfather took the paper and looked at it. "Yes,"

he said. "I know this firm. They make nothing but uniforms." Then he looked at me and said: "But you're too small."

And to this my grandmother again added, this time emphatically: "And too young!"

But I was determined. "They have my size," I said. "I'm taller than Tommy Schultz and Bobby Wilder."

"They have his size," my grandfather said quietly to my grandmother. And I could tell from his remark that my battle was won.

"Tomorrow," I said. "I can get home early from school and we can go to Cooper Square. They have all kinds of uniforms, but, Grandfather, just ask for the P.S.18 Cadets. It's a blue coat with a row of brass buttons down the middle. Every button has an eagle stamped on it. And the trousers have a broad white stripe down the sides. The hat has a leather peak. You can't make a mistake. I know exactly the right one!"

That is how I became a cadet in the very week that the *Maine* was blown up in Havana harbor.

Every afternoon at three o'clock when school was over we cadets assembled. We marched.

In bad weather we marched up and down the basement corridors. In good weather we marched in the yard. At first there were only fourteen in our company. But with the flames of war being fanned by the newspapers our number soon grew to twenty-two. Day after day, in our military uniforms, we marched up and down the basement corridors and the school yard until we wearied of the place. The monotony became unbearable. And, besides, the place was not big enough for twenty-two eager cadets. There were too many walls. Each day the space between the walls seemed to grow more narrow. Our marching seemed to be reduced to nothing but "Mark time," "Halt," and "About face." Something had to be done.

One fine spring afternoon our captain, whose name was Reinhardt, and whose authority was proudly marked with a belt and sword, boldly marched us out into the street. The sight of the open space revived our spirits. And over and over again we went up and down the middle of Fifty-first Street in front of the brewery that was opposite our school.

This new parade ground seemed very good at first, but we soon got tangled up with brewery wagons and horses and were forced to retreat. We left Fifty-first Street and marched around the corner to Park Avenue on the block of the Steinway piano factory. Things were a lot better here. There were no brewery wagons and horses.

But there were other disadvantages to Park Avenue. The noise of the trains in the open cut and the noise of the piano factory often drowned out the commands of our captain. And Park Avenue was the hangout of rowdies, gangs, and hobos! But since we were twenty-two strong and wore a uniform very like that of the Civil War heroes, we decided to risk these dangers, for on Park Avenue there was plenty of room.

Day after day we marched up and down in front of the piano factory. But it was not long before we also began to tire of this new parade ground. Then one memorable afternoon Captain Reinhardt took a bold step and marched us into foreign territory. He led us on to one of the long wooden bridges that spanned the broad railroad cut. We were heading for the far side of Park Avenue. And it was then that a wonderful thing happened. We were just half-way across the bridge when a big steam train puffing hard happened to pass under us. Suddenly we were enveloped in a thick cloud of black smoke and steam.

"Halt!" cried our captain, drawing his sword.

We stopped. The whole world was blotted out.

"Hold firm, men!" Reinhardt cried.

We could not see our captain, but we heard his voice through the steam and smoke. We knew that he was still with us. It was wonderful! When the smoke and steam cleared, there in the middle of the bridge stood twenty-two battle-scarred veterans.

Now the game was clear. Reinhardt and his two officers, a sergeant and a corporal, surveyed the field for good north-bound or southbound trains. Once a train was discovered, we would march bravely to the proper position on the bridge and wait for the attack.

"Here she comes, men," our captain would cry, drawing his sword. "Get ready. And hold firm."

Then with a pounding, a rush, and a clatter the engine would pass beneath us and envelop us in a heavy cloud. We would stand firm until the steam and smoke dispersed, then march on to a fresh battle position.

That evening when I got back to the cigar store Grandpa looked at me and said: "Your face is black as coal. Where have you been?"

"Battle practice," I said.

Day after day we cadets marched up and down Park Avenue and across the bridges battling with the steam trains, until we began to tire of this too. Then our captain looked abroad for something new. And he found just what we needed. He found a blacksmith's shop not far from our school. It was a big shop with three ringing anvils. And there were always a number of horses waiting to be shod. Now, each day, after we had had our fill of Park Avenue and the trains, Captain Reinhardt would march us down to the blacksmith's shop.

"Company halt!" he would cry out.

Then he alone would advance and survey the forges. When he saw a number of shoes glowing red hot in the flames he would come back to us and order us to mark time. This was in preparation for the ordeal by fire that was to come. As soon as the glowing shoes were lifted from the forges on to the anvils and the blacksmiths started to hammer, we received the command "Advance!" And Reinhardt with his sword aloft would lead us forward through a great shower of sparks.

In these ways did we march and harden ourselves for battle in the early months of the year 1898.

After two exciting months of marching we cadets began to worry. War had still not been declared. Dark thoughts filled our minds. Was the President really going to find a way to avoid war? Were we going to be denied the right to fight for our country? Was Spain going to get away with it?

But just when our plight seemed the most desperate the

sun shone out in full. Congress declared war. And no sooner
was war declared than the whole city took on a livelier
aspect. Flags appeared as from nowhere, people talked a lot
more, and every evening just after the workers got home and
began settling down for a little rest and quiet the newspapers brought out an extra edition.

Every night at seven or eight o'clock newsboys went
through the streets crying "Yextra! Yextra! Read all about
it!" Their cries could be heard two blocks off, and everyone
had plenty of time to prepare. As the newsboys came down
the streets people came out of every house, bought their
papers and hurried back to "read all about it." And no one
was ever disappointed, for the press always found a good
subject to write about—something that could be discussed
all evening long and even next morning at breakfast. Yes,
there was no doubt about it: with America at war, the city
was a livelier place.

We cadets entered into the spirit of things by extending
our marches. We no longer limited ourselves to Park Avenue and the neighborhood blocks. We tramped day after
day through miles and miles of the city streets past endless
rows of brownstone houses. And we were not alone. Occasionally we ran across veterans of the Civil War, members
of the Grand Army of the Republic, who had ideas similar
to ours. They had got out their old uniforms and were also
marching!

Then one day we heard the news that the President had
called for volunteers. This was just what we had been waiting
for. But before we had time to formulate a plan Theodore
Roosevelt blazed into the news. It seemed that Roosevelt,

who had formerly been Commissioner of our New York
police force and had lived for some years on a ranch in the
territory of Dakota, was organizing a regiment of Rough
Riders. These Rough Riders were made up of our best western cowboys and a stabilizing group of millionaires and society men from Long Island and Fifth Avenue. It was then
that we cadets of P.S.18 knew for certain that Spain had no
chance. For who was there in the whole world who could
stand up against our cowboys? Especially when they were
backed up by everything that money could buy. How we
wished we could join with these riders! But none of us had
ever been on a horse, except perhaps an old brewery-wagon
horse that was being led around the corner to the blacksmith shop. Some of us had had free rides on such horses,
but our feet had never touched stirrups.

Still we marched. We knew that the Rough Riders would
go first, but later, we were certain, our turn would come.
Cuba would be freed, and in this crusade we would help.

We counted the long days until we should be needed.
Never had time passed more slowly. Finally Reinhardt could
bear it no longer. One day he took me aside and told me of
a plan he had devised. He said that down on Third Avenue,
in a vacant store, the Army had opened up a recruiting office.

"Let's go," he said. "It looks like rain, so we can't march
anyway this afternoon."

I looked up at the sky. The spring sun was shining
brightly. But if Reinhardt said it was going to rain. . . .
After all, he was captain and I was only a private.

"Sure," I said. "Let's go."

"After school," he said.

"But how about the others?"

"That's the whole idea," he said. "You and I will join up first. Then we will find a way to get the others in. If our whole company goes down at one time, then maybe no one will get in."

Reinhardt's reasoning seemed sound to me.

All day Reinhardt and I waited impatiently for the three-o'clock bell to ring. Then we ran down into the yard, and Reinhardt announced to one of his officers: "Tell 'em no marching today. It's going to rain."

The next minute the two of us started off down Third Avenue as fast as we could go, to the recruiting station.

"You are sure it's down this way?" I asked.

"Yep. It's way down near Forty-second Street. I know where."

At length we came to the place. It was an empty store with posters outside. Some men were inside. At a table sat a sergeant. He wore a broad-brimmed felt hat, and his ruddy face was decorated with a large reddish handle-bar mustache. He was talking with a man, and we waited for him to finish.

Finally we stepped forward and saluted. He looked up and examined us carefully. Then he leaned back in his chair and said: "Who are youse?"

"P.S.18 Cadets, sir," said Reinhardt.

I nodded, for on such occasions I tried to avoid talking. I stammered anyway, and at times like this my stammer was at its worst.

"And what do youse want?"

"Go to Cuba. Enlist," said Reinhardt.

"Youse boys want enlist? Is that it?"

"Yes, sir."

"How old are youse?"

Reinhardt did not reply, and I spoke up as best I could. "Going on nine, sir," I said. I did not want to say I was only eight. I felt sure that nine would sound a lot better.

The sergeant scratched his head, then he said: "What kind of uniforms youse boys got, anyway?"

We were embarrassed and did not know how to reply.

"Lemme see that cap of yours."

I took off my cap and handed it to him.

"Looks like the Grand Army of the Republic."

" 'Tis not," said Reinhardt boldly. "We are P.S.18 Cadets. Everybody in New York knows that."

"How would everybody know that?"

"We march every year in the Decoration Day parade."

"Youse do?" he said, surprised. And he seemed pleased.

Then I added: "Yes, sir, we do." But I did not tell him I was a new cadet and had not yet marched in this parade.

Now Reinhardt added: "If you saw the parade last year, sir, then you saw us."

"All right. Now youse want to go to Cuba?"

We smiled and nodded hopefully.

"And what would youse do in Cuba?"

"Fight the enemy," said Reinhardt, and I nodded in full agreement.

The sergeant looked at us seriously. He seemed to be considering the whole situation. Then he asked: "Exactly what can youse do?"

"We can drum," I said quickly. "We can carry water and coffee to the men."

"Can youse bugle?"

"No, sir."

"But we can run dispatches," I added. "And we are fast. You can try us and see. Aren't we fast?" I appealed to Reinhardt.

"Sure. No one can beat us."

Here the matter rested, and we waited for the sergeant to give his verdict. He could see the plea in our eyes.

"Youse boys is too young," he announced.

"We're not young," said Reinhardt.

"Go home," said the sergeant.

"But we want to go to Cuba," I said.

"Come back next year."

"The Rough Riders," said Reinhardt, "will finish them off. And next year it will be too late."

"Youse is too young. Go home! Youse heard what I said."

This was final. And from this decision we felt there could be no appeal. We walked back up Third Avenue with sad and heavy hearts. And we agreed never to tell anyone that we had been to the recruiting office. The humiliation of our rejection was too much to confess.

Every morning at nine o'clock it was the duty of the cadets to bring the American flag into the assembly hall. This was done to the tune of a lively march played by our music teacher on an old square piano. We would wait in the outer corridor until the rolling doors that divided the assembly hall into classrooms were all rolled back and everything was ready. Then when Dr. Kieran, our principal, mounted the platform and the loose-stringed piano began to sound, we marched along the back of the hall and down the center aisle carrying the flag.

After the entire school had pledged allegiance to the flag we placed it in its stand beside the platform and found our seats. The music teacher would then announce the song that we were to sing and play a sample chord to give us the key. And we would sing in high, shrill voices that could be heard in the brewery across the street and in the Steinway piano factory around the corner.

After the last note of the song had died Dr. Kieran would rise from his chair and, stepping forward, open the big Bible on the lectern. Each day he would read a long passage from the Old Testament. Because of the great mixture of races and religious beliefs in New York, the New Testament was never read in the public schools.

Dr. Kieran had a wonderful reading voice, deep, rich, and sonorous. It seemed to fit the language of the Bible. This was different from the language we used in daily life. And yet we understood it well. It seemed a language especially reserved for those stories of long, long ago. These ancient stories seemed wonderful to me because they were filled with struggle and filled with hope. They had in them real drama. And they also had cruelty, revenge, and hatred. And here and there was a touch of magic and supernatural wonder.

I liked it when the waves of the sea parted and a whole multitude marched safely through. I liked it when Jonah rode in the belly of a whale and Daniel walked into the lions' den. These tales lingered in my imagination. And I thought it real magic when Aaron threw his staff to the ground and it became a live serpent.

Many times I tried this trick myself in the backyard behind the store. I would hurl a stick to the ground and wait and watch. But nothing ever happened. I finally concluded that I lacked the right touch for that kind of thing. And it made me feel inferior. But then I consoled myself, for what would I have done with a wiggling snake in the backyard?

I liked the story about Joseph, who was sold by his brothers and later became very powerful, and all his brothers had to ask his forgiveness. And I liked the idea very much of the woman turned into a pillar of salt, and Jacob's ladder that went up into the sky, and the young boy with a slingshot killing the ugly giant, and Samson so strong that he pulled down the whole Temple.

All these were wonderful tales, and as I sat there listening to Dr. Kieran read from the Bible I was transported into a mythical land. And I felt myself part of every story.

Dressed in my blue cadet uniform with its long row of brass buttons, I imagined myself a warrior in some ancient army fighting and vanquishing every evil in the whole world. And I was sorry when the reading was done, the Bible closed, and the doors rolled back again, dividing the hall into its classrooms.

Then I was back once more in the world of reality, the world of arithmetic and spelling—things that were bothersome and required the mind of a wizard. And one also had to study geography. One had to study large maps of the world that showed far-off places. It was all so dreary!

And I could never see what need we had of those faraway

places when we were so lucky to live on an enchanted isle
with steamboats, gypsies, trains, tigers, everything that was
exciting. Who cared about the products of Brazil? Who
cared about the wines of France? I never paid attention to
such dull things; at least, not until this year, the year in
which the *Maine* was blown up.

But now, suddenly, everything seemed different. Other islands beyond my own island became important. And the
maps that had formerly seemed so useless and dreary took
on life and color. War had made this difference.

First of all we children wanted to know where Cuba was.
And we were surprised to learn that Cuba was also an island,
only much larger than the one on which we lived. We were
anxious to locate it, for somehow or other we now had special interests there. We found out about the people of Cuba
and the produce of the land.

At the front of our classroom we had large maps of Europe, Asia, Africa, and the United States. We also had a
map of the world. These maps were like window shades,
and they were attached to the top of the blackboards. We
asked our teacher so many questions that the big map of the
world was often pulled down for half a day. There were a
lot of events that had suddenly come into the news, and
a lot of places besides Cuba had to be located.

First of all we had to find the Philippines, for all of us
knew that President McKinley had sent a sharp cable to
Commodore Dewey to sail at once for Manila, find the Spanish fleet, and blow it to bits. This was an appealing idea, and
we had to find the place where this explosion would occur.

We also wanted to locate the Hawaiian Islands, for our government had just signed a special treaty of annexation with the people of these islands.

Then we were also interested in seeing where Panama was, because there was a lot of talk about digging a canal across the Isthmus.

On the map that narrow little strip of land that joins North and South America seemed like just nothing at all. I felt that with a good shovel I could dig the canal myself. But our teacher explained to us that the French government had been working on this project for years and that, what with the tropical heat, the jungles, and the yellow fever, they had been unable to finish it. Now President McKinley had appointed a commission to investigate the possibility of taking over this job from the French, and things might soon be humming.

As we studied the map of the world we noticed that many places were printed in red. Wherever one looked there were big blotches of red. Canada was red, Australia and India were red, a good part of Africa was red, the British Isles were also red, and there were red splotches in Asia and South America. All this was the British Empire. No wonder people said that the sun never set on the lands of Britain. And all this was ruled by Queen Victoria. At this time Victoria was almost eighty years old. She was quite an old lady. But my, what a lot of land she had! And what a big navy and army she had compared to ours!

If at that time someone had come to me and said that I should live to see the day when most of the vast British Empire would be dissolved, I should have thought him just plain crazy. Nothing in the world seemed more permanent than the British Empire. And our United States looked very small on the map of the world compared with it. I was quite envious; I thought that the English had too much.

After asking all the questions we could about the British Empire our eyes again came back to Cuba, to the Philippines, and to a vast yellow expanse that was China. Here we had a special interest, the city of Peking. For this place too had suddenly come into our lives. It seemed that halfway around the world in this city of Peking there was trouble. The Chinese had suddenly developed a hatred for foreigners, and they were threatening American missionaries and Europeans living in Peking. We read all about this in the newspapers, and New York was alive with stories.

It was easy to believe all kinds of horrible things about the Chinese, because, to begin with, they did not look like us, and that was bad. They had yellow skin, slanting eyes, and long pigtails. Then they dressed in a very peculiar fashion; their women did not wear corsets and big hats with ostrich plumes, their men did not wear starched collars, and there was not a necktie in the whole of China. There was no question about it, they were a strange people, and it was well known that most of them had leprosy and smoked opium. In fact, it was pretty well known that a large part of their population were opium fiends. All this we had been told, and we believed it to be true. We found it very easy to believe such things about people we did not know.

As we sat in our classroom looking at the map of China, our minds were filled with these stories, and we were not at all surprised when our teacher told us that this great territory in the East was ruled over by a strict old woman who smoked opium. The Empress Tzu-hsi was at this time about sixty-five years old. How strange, I thought, that two old disagreeable women should have control of the greater part of the world! And I felt that it was a lucky thing that the United States had two big oceans, the Atlantic and the Pacific, to separate us from these two old ladies.

The map of the world had suddenly become very interesting. The eyes of the American people now turned to far-off places. It was not just the people living in New York who had suddenly become aware of the world about them: all America was learning geography. I know this for a fact because the book salesmen who went from door to door selling sets of books now featured a world atlas. And over the United States at this period many thousands of these atlases were sold. Now for the first time many of us learned where Europe was and where Asia lay among the world continents.

As I studied the map of the world I was struck by the jagged shore line of the continents and the odd shapes the land created. And I noticed that there was a definite tendency for land to hang down, droop and trail off into the sea. California, Florida, Nova Scotia, Italy, Spain, Scandinavia, Malaya, Greenland, India, Korea, Kamchatka, North America, ending at Panama, South America, and Alaska—everything seemed to hang down; everything except perhaps perky little Denmark. Why the lands of the world trailed off toward the south I could not understand. And to this day I still do not know.

There was another thing about the map of the world that

interested me. Here and there were great white blotches that fired my imagination. These blank spaces represented the unexplored areas of the different continents. Most of them were in Central Africa, but some were in South America and Central Asia. A great part of Tibet was blank, as well as the sources of the Nile and of the Amazon. Central Persia and Western Mongolia were also white patches. So many places of the world were still unexplored and uncharted!

And I wanted to know why nobody had ever been to these places and if anyone was planning to do something about it. I thought to myself that maybe some day I might go to some of these blank spots and come home a great hero and discoverer.

I asked lots of questions of my teachers. But they were indifferent to places so far away, and they were unable to answer me. In fact, they seemed to resent my interest in what was unknown and uncharted. They thought it would be better if I stuck to such known facts as spelling and arithmetic. They had little or no understanding of a child's imaginative curiosity, and they made one feel that knowledge should have strict boundaries and could be implanted by a question-and-answer method as in a catechism. They seemed to have great respect for the printed word, and the book answer was always considered the correct one. What was not contained in a book was never to be pried into. In this way did ignorance protect itself and maintain its authority.

But this stifling attitude of my teachers did not curb my curiosity, although I feel certain that it did destroy the curiosity of many of my classmates. Through the years I con-

tinued asking questions and seeking answers. And in the
end, through curiosity, I learned a great many things that
enriched my life. I can truthfully say that I learned more by
myself through the pursuit of my curiosity than I ever
learned from any teacher during the years of my schooling.

While in school we were studying the charts of the world
and I was dreaming of the unexplored regions, our war in
Cuba was doing fine. It was one of the best wars ever. Theodore Roosevelt and his Rough Riders were taking things in
hand. He was a New York boy, and we had great confidence
in him.

As for Commodore Dewey, he had carried out the instructions of the President. He had sailed his battleships into
Manila Harbor and blown the Spanish fleet to bits. And
only six Americans had been slightly wounded. This, of
course, is how a war should be fought. And everyone had
been very much pleased when, about a week later, Dewey
was made a Rear Admiral.

But, besides the war in Cuba, we in New York were able
to enjoy another war, a private one. This war was between
two powerful newspapers, Hearst's *Journal* and Pulitzer's
World. It was a war that went on day and night. It was a
war that was fought for special dispatches, headlines, edi-
torials, and circulation. And because of my advantageous
position as the grandson of a man who ran an agency, I was
able to witness at close range many of the battles down on
Park Row.

Each evening when Grandpa and I went downtown to
deliver the advertisements, we went from one newspaper

office to the other. We saw everything. We heard everything. But we were very tactful, and we never told the *World* that we had just come from the *Journal*. Night after night we found the offices of these two rival newspapers humming with mad excitement. The air was charged with tension. One expected an explosion at any moment.

In the battle for headlines each paper tried to outdo the other. Events were first dramatized, then made sensational, and finally made catastrophic. The newspapers had special boys whose job it was to get each edition of the rival paper hot off the press. If the *Journal* announced an encounter in bold type, then the *World* would make it a heated skirmish in bolder type, and an hour later the *Journal* would again report it all as a bloody battle.

I often watched the men who wrote the headlines (what I called the big words) and also those who wrote the copy. And I tried hard to discover how news was manufactured— how nothing was made into something, and how this something was given importance. Very often the headline had little or nothing to do with the article that followed. Very often the articles and headlines had nothing to do with the truth. I didn't think it quite honest; yet the men who manufactured the news were friendly and nice. I liked them. It was all a strange business and it mystified me.

Besides the war for headlines, there was also a war for circulation. Each paper had its own wagons and its own gang of newsboys. Sometimes two rival wagons started racing uptown, each determined to beat the other with the extra. As the bundles were dropped off at the corner newsstands the wagons grew lighter and the horses made better speed. Each wagon carried a driver and two bundle boys. The wagons maneuvered for position. Each tried to cut off the other. Each claimed the right of way. And often at a convenient place the crew of one wagon attacked the crew of the other wagon. Those who suffered defeat swore revenge. In this way rivalry grew into violence. But the police did not interfere. They recognized that this was a private war.

When the clashes between the wagon crews became too frequent the newspapers hired gangsters to ride along to protect them. Those who were wounded in the fray were brought back to the newspaper buildings, where special cots were set up in the basements. Doctors were constantly on hand to stitch up the open gashes.

All that spring we marched.

We marched across the Park Avenue bridges right through the hot engine steam and smoke. We marched through the showers of sparks that flew from the blacksmith's hammers. We also marched far afield down strange streets in other parts of the city. And all the time Reinhardt and I shared a secret.

Now and then we consulted with each other. The recruiting sergeant had told us to come back next year. This was a long time to wait.

"My birthday is in September," I said. "Then I will be a year older."

"Mine is in October," said Reinhardt.

"That should count for a year."

"I guess so."

Therefore we decided that after the summer vacation we would go back to the recruiting office and tell the sergeant that we were both a year older and that now everything was all right.

Reinhardt said that during the summer he would try to practice on a bugle or a cornet so that the army would have no possible excuse to refuse him. I promised to practice running and all those things expected of a dispatch runner. I considered myself particularly well suited for this kind of work.

How we managed to get through the first part of the summer I do not recall, but we did. All this time my uniform hung in the closet. Now and again I would open the closet door to make sure that it was still there.

And several times when I was down at Newspaper Row I would ask the men: "Mister, could you tell me how long does a war last?"

"You want to know how long a war lasts?"

"Yes, sir."

"Hard to say. Did you never hear of the Thirty Years' War?"

"No, sir."

"And how long was the Civil War?"

"I don't know exactly."

"Well, I'll tell you and then you will know.

In 1861 the war begun,
In 1862 the Yankees pushed it through,
In 1863 the Negro was free,
And in 1864 the war was o'er
And Johnny came marching home."

"Four years," I said. "That's good."

"What's good about it?"

"I don't know. It's just good. They promised to take me next year."

"They did?"

"Yep."

"You better grow some."

"I will, sir."

But we could not wait until school reopened. There was too much excitement going on in Cuba. In July we heard of more Spanish ships blasted out of the waters around Santiago harbor. And so with all this going on Reinhardt and I figured we must have grown quite a bit and we would try again.

We got our uniforms out of moth balls and again journeyed down Third Avenue to Forty-second Street.

On the way down Reinhardt seemed worried. "Supposing the man with the big red mustache is not there?" he asked.

"Well, then there will be another sergeant and we can talk to him."

"But he would not know what had been promised, would he?"

"No. But we would tell him."

"He might not believe us. We should have got a paper or something we could show."

"If the U.S. Army promises something, they are not going to go back on their word, are they?" I argued.

"No," admitted Reinhardt.

At length we arrived at the spot, and, alas, there was no recruiting station to be found. The empty store had been rented and was now a grocery. We went inside and asked the shopkeeper, but he did not know anything about a recruiting station. We came out and found a policeman.

"Was one here once," he said. "Closed up. Don't need 'em any more. They got more volunteers than they can use."

This was a terrible blow.

But still Reinhardt and I had hopes. I explained to him that the Civil War had lasted four years and that I had even heard of a war that lasted thirty years. These were real facts. And from such facts we took encouragement.

But the encouragement did not last long.

In August, about a month before school opened, we heard the sad news that our troops were being sent out of Cuba in a hurry. Yellow fever and food poisoning had set in and the fighting was over. A truce was signed, and Roosevelt and his Rough Riders had become the heroes of the day.

That Roosevelt should emerge as a hero was no surprise to us who lived in New York. Any officer of our police force was certain to display unusual bravery and leadership. We all knew before Roosevelt ever put his foot on Cuban soil that he and the cowboys and millionaires who were with him were bound to do something great. If there was nothing great handy, they would surely make something great and conquer it. Someone trained on the New York police force, we firmly believed, could conquer anything.

And they conquered everything so terrifically that the war was over before it hardly began.

When school opened in September our cadets assembled and we did march, but we marched without spirit. We were sad.

But toward the end of the year our hopes were suddenly revived. More trouble was brewing in other places in the world. All was not lost.

In the first few months of 1899, after the independence of the Philippine Islands was declared, the Filipinos rose up in revolt. And on the day that we heard that 70,000 U.S. soldiers were sailing to put down the Filipino resistance we again marched across the bridges, through the smoke and through the blacksmith's shower of sparks. Our old spirit was back. Once more we were hardening ourselves for battle.

And in this year of 1899, we cadets had still more reason to feel encouraged, for those two old disagreeable women who ruled the world got into trouble.

Queen Victoria had trouble in South Africa and was sending troops to fight the Dutch settlers. The Boer War was on. This, of course, did not involve the United States. However, we liked it, for it added to the general excitement of the time. And everyone, especially the Irish, took sides. The Irish saloons in our neighborhood displayed the Dutch flag just to show what they thought of England.

But with that other old woman, the Dowager Empress of China, there was real trouble that did concern America. This old opium-smoking fiend, as we truly believed her to be, was encouraging an evil society of yellow devils who were making life uncomfortable for all the American missionaries, Europeans, and everyone else of the white race in China. The Empress supported this society, which called itself "The Order of Literary Patriotic Harmonious Fists." They believed in striking out with their fists. And for that reason our newspapers named them the Boxers.

Although the Empress and the Boxers had as yet done nothing very wrong, everyone felt that there was serious trouble ahead. Our newspapers did their best to keep things very warm; month after month they fought a war with China all by themselves. Every night we had extras about either the Philippines, Victoria's war with the Boers, or the storm clouds gathering over China.

There was excitement everywhere, on the streets, in the homes, and in our schools. Journalism had at last come into a golden age. With disaster piled on disaster the newspapers were making fortunes. Magazines, too, were now printing lively articles. Even a little obscure weekly called *The Saturday Evening Post,* which only two years before had been sold in Philadelphia for $1000, was now seen on all newsstands. Between our own wars and the bungling of the two disagreeable Empresses, journalism was truly thriving. In fact, it was thriving so well and keeping everything so much alive that we felt that we were living in a wonderful world. A world of excitement; a world made for heroes.

But even before we could go to war we had to march in the Victory Parade. It was Reinhardt who announced it to me, and at first I thought he was joking. But no. It was true. Admiral Dewey, commanding a Navy flotilla, was headed at full steam for New York harbor. And here, on our enchanted island, Admiral Dewey would have the greatest welcome that any American hero could ever have. For who in the entire history of the United States had ever before sunk a whole enemy fleet?

Yes, there was going to be a victory parade, and we cadets of P.S.18 were listed to march with the U.S. Army and Navy. This we felt was only right, for though we had not got to Cuba we had been ready to go at the first call, and what is more, thanks to the smoke and steam supplied gratis by the New York Central Railroad and the blacksmith's showers of sparks we were truly battle-hardened.

The biggest loving cup I ever saw in my life was displayed in the window of a Fifth Avenue jeweler. It was about four feet tall, so big around that I could have crept inside, and made of solid silver. It was a present to Admiral Dewey from the people of the City of New York.

And this was not all that the city was doing for Admiral Dewey. Every important sculptor in New York—there were about twenty-five or thirty—was on a committee to build the biggest plaster of Paris victory arch in the whole world. In fact, it was more than an arch, and week after week we boys went down to Madison Square to watch it take form. It was certainly the most beautiful thing we had ever seen.

The arch itself, about two or three stories high, was constructed in the square at Twenty-third Street where Fifth Avenue crosses Broadway. And leading into the arch for a block or more on either side were sets of Greek columns. Four columns were grouped together in each set, and on the top of each column was a big plaster ball. At the base of each set of columns were large, more than life-size figures of angels with their wings spread and plaster palm branches in their outstretched hands.

The parade was set for September 30. Crowds of people

from all states in the Union began arriving in the city. Vendors sold Dewey buttons, American flags, and guidebooks.

These guidebooks listed all the places of interest in the city as well as the many hotels and boardinghouses. But my grandfather thought the prices were too high. Most hotels were charging $2.50 a day with meals. And two hotels, the Waldorf and the Astor House, were charging $2.50 a day without meals! The boardinghouses had also raised their prices from $1.00 to $1.50 a day with meals.

My grandfather said: "They're taking advantage of visitors. It's not right. It's like charging ten cents for a five-cent cigar."

And it was Mr. Hadley who said: "How can a man pay out $1.50 a day when he only earns $2.00 a day? That's the standard price for labor."

"I can well remember," said my grandfather, "when a laboring man got only a dollar."

"Industry did not give the workingman that extra dollar willingly," said Mr. Hadley. "It was the high cost of living that brought it about. And I can see a day coming when labor will earn $3.00 a day."

Grandpa thought $3.00 much too much. He shook his head. "No," he said. "Sooner than pay a man that kind of fancy wages industry can import labor from Europe."

Mr. Hadley laughed. "Sure. That is what they have been doing right along. Unless labor in America has brains enough to organize it will be squeezed out of existence."

My grandfather did not like this kind of talk. He thought it was socialism, and that was something very bad.

But in spite of the high cost of rooms and food the crowds

that came to New York were merry and gay. In the evening everyone strolled down Fifth Avenue to see the show-window displays of all the tokens in gold and silver that were going to be presented to Admiral Dewey. These were gifts from numerous patriotic societies. And everyone agreed that the Admiral would need a wagon to take it all home.

The day before the parade there was a great naval display on the Hudson River. And those of us who made up the crowds that lined Riverside Drive saw a wonderful flotilla of Navy vessels, belching heavy smoke, steam up the river bringing Admiral Dewey to our city. Two famous yachts, one belonging to J. P. Morgan and the other to the well-known English sportsman and tea merchant, Sir Thomas Lipton, led the way. Behind the trim white yachts followed units of the U.S. battle fleet—the battleships *Iowa, Indiana, Massachusetts, Oregon,* and *Texas,* and with them the cruisers *New York* and *Brooklyn.* They steamed up the river in single file, and when each of the vessels came opposite Grant's Tomb it fired a tremendous salute. Each salvo rocked the earth and made us feel the great power of our navy. We knew that it was with such fine salvos that the Spanish fleet had been blown to bits.

Everyone thought this a wonderful sight except Mr. Hadley, who came into the cigar store late that afternoon. "Why should millionaires' yachts lead the U.S. Navy?"

"It was an honor guard," said my grandfather.

"The Navy needs no honor from rich men. Who does the Navy belong to anyway, the American people or the millionaires? Admiral Dewey should not have allowed it." Mr. Hadley seemed quite angry about the whole matter. He stuffed his pipe nervously, lit it with quick puffs, and marched out.

But regardless of what Mr. Hadley thought, that night the streets of the city were filled with crowds and with sailors on shore leave. They sang and danced, and many got drunk, and some had fights. But everyone was happy, and even those who fought had a good time.

The next day I was up very early. I joined the cadets gathered in front of the school building, and as soon as the roll was called we all piled into one of the large brewery wagons provided by the brewery across the street. The wagon was decorated with red, white, and blue bunting and American flags. The horses, fine big Belgian horses, wore red, white, and blue bonnets with holes to allow their long ears to stick through. They seemed to sense the holiday and, pleased to find their wagon so light, they trotted happily all the way to the place where the parade was to begin.

Although we were early, the side streets were already beginning to fill with men and boys from different Army and Navy units and civilian groups. There were companies of Civil War veterans, sailors, members of the National Guard, boys from public and parochial schools, West Point cadets, and cadets from other distinguished military academies. Some of these units had brass bands, and the parade officials were busy arranging the marching order so that the bands would be well spaced and the music of one band would not conflict with that of another.

While this shuffling was going on our captain, Reinhardt, and the two brewery wagon drivers, who on this day were dressed in their Sunday suits and derby hats, went about maneuvering for position. At length they came back waving their arms with excitement. "We found them Zouaves!" they called. "Hurry!"

"Come on, boys! That's the place for youse," called one of the drivers.

Sure enough, the famous Zouaves were lined up two blocks away. We lost no time, but fell in line right behind them.

"Dis is a good place," said one of the drivers.

"Stay here, boys," said the other, "and ask no questions from nobody. Youse got no band anyway, so they can't move youse around. And when the Zouaves march out, youse march out right behind 'em. And don't let nobody hook your place. Our Fifty-foist Street boys is as good as any, see."

This was indeed a fine place to be, for the New York Fire Zouaves were a very famous and colorful regiment, one of the most famous and certainly the most colorful of all the regiments of the Grand Army of the Republic. Their costume had been modeled after that of the French Zouaves in Algeria. It consisted of loose red Turkish trousers, a jacket of blue with fancy edging, a sky-blue silk sash, white gaiters, and a Turkish fez for a hat.

This fancy-dress costume would have created a comic effect had not the Zouaves earned the reputation of being terrific fighters. Most of the men now had grizzly beards, but they carried daggers in their silk sashes, and they had with them their bullet-riddled and bloodstained battle flags.

We lined up behind them at a respectful distance. But one of the wagon drivers came up and said: "Get in close, so no bums take dis place away from youse." We moved up a pace or two and held our position. And, sure enough, there were some who tried to squeeze in. But we held firm, and the brewery men protected us. In their derby hats smartly tilted to one side they stood guard and said: "Dese is the Fifty-foist Street Cadets. Dere's plenty room behind 'em. Dese cadets is wid the Zouaves."

And that is how it was. We marched behind the famous Zouaves. And all along the way there was a shower of applause, which we enjoyed even though it was intended for the bearded heroes of the Civil War. We basked in their glory.

Several hours later, when we reached the Dewey Arch, we were exhausted. But we kept our heads up, our chins in, and our line straight. We marched the very best we could. And soon we were passing the grandstand, filled with all sorts of distinguished people. This was the big moment. We battle-hardened cadets from P.S.18 were passing in review.

But there were so many plumed admirals' hats and so much glittering gold braid that later not one of us could say for certain that he had seen Admiral Dewey. Not one of us was really sure. But I am certain that Admiral Dewey was there and that he saw us.

For a long time we had looked forward to this day, and now it was over. We were tired. We were hungry. Fortunately the brewery wagon was waiting for us at the end of the march to drive us back to Fifty-first Street.

Besides being tired and hungry we were all a little sad. This victory parade meant the end of war. The whole world would now live in peace. We who had marched so hard and so long would never again have a chance. We somehow felt that we had been cheated. But we were wrong. For the very next year the trouble that had long been brewing in China finally broke out.

One day the Empress ordered closed the gates of the walled city of Peking. This meant only one thing to us: It meant that all the white people inside Peking were trapped. And we felt sure that it was only a matter of time before "The Order of Literary Patriotic Harmonious Fists" would break out with a massacre.

All this horrible news came to us through our newspapers. The dispatches were never too clear on what was going on in Peking, but it did not really matter. Everyone could easily imagine what was taking place, and all of us got really worked up against the Chinese. Every day we had extra editions and big black headlines. And we all sat on edge and waited.

At last good news came.

A rescue party was on its way. This force, we were told, consisted of 2,500 Americans, 3,000 British, 800 French, and 8,000 Japanese. All were moving in on the walled city of Peking. But could they possibly reach the city in time to effect a rescue? Everyone who came into the cigar store had an opinion on the subject.

"What does a Chink know about boxing, anyway?" asked one.

And Mrs. O'Leary was certain that "Them Chinese people is the cruelest people in the world. They've got more tortures than there are in hell. And I'll tell you what I think, and mark me words. They will torture the white people and wait. They will wait until our soldiers are knocking down the doors in their Chinee wall, and then they will slit the throats of every man, woman, and child. You just mark me words."

Then again, very suddenly, everything was over and the Boxer Rebellion was ended. In fact, it was over in just a few days.

But exactly what happened in Peking nobody really knew, because our newspaper accounts were all so confusing. That is, we never really knew exactly what happened in Peking until several months later when Buffalo Bill came to Madison Square Garden with his Wild West Show. Then we saw, and we understood.

Buffalo Bill, whose real name was William F. Cody, always opened the show by riding into the arena on a white pony. Under his western sombrero he had a grayish Vandyke beard. He wore a buckskin jacket with a fringed edge. His trousers, too, were buckskin, and he had laced leggings. As he rode around the arena he waved his hat to the applauding crowd. Behind him followed a long line of Indians in full feathered regalia and any number of bronco-busting cowboys and sharpshooting cowgirls in leggings and short skirts.

Always in former years the act that concluded the show had been a presentation of Custer's Last Fight. But this year Buffalo Bill presented a re-enactment of the Boxer Rebellion.

After all the sharpshooting, Indian races, bronco-busting, and roping acts were finished the lights of the Garden were dimmed and, while the audience waited and the orchestra played soft music, special scenery was put together at one end of the arena.

When the lights came on again we saw an amazing sight: a replica of the Peking wall, complete with a great closed gate and a backdrop of Chinese buildings and tiled roofs. Along the top of the wall marched Chinese soldiers in yellow silk mandarin coats, carrying poles on which were mounted very fancy battle-axes. Long black braided pigtails hung down their backs. And here and there at their feet reclined Chinamen with devilish faces, smoking opium pipes.

Slowly the lights were again dimmed, and we all waited. The Garden was still as night. Then the quiet was broken by the clear sound of a distant bugle. This was soon followed by the roll of drums and the pound of horses' hoofs. The Americans were coming!

Now a lone scout rode cautiously into the arena. He looked about nervously, dismounted, and crept forward on his stomach. When he reached a certain point he turned his head and signaled with a long waving arm.

The music grew louder. The horses' hoofs grew louder. On top of the wall the Chinese soldiers set up the alarm and started running back and forth just to make activity. The opium smokers, in a drunken stupor, took fright and joined the soldiers, causing great confusion. It was easy to see that between stupidity and degeneracy things were in bad shape on top of the Peking wall.

And just when the Chinese were the most confused the first American soldier entered the battle zone. He rode into the arena at full gallop, carrying a large silk American flag upon which the spotlight glared. There was a shower of applause. But this was soon drowned out by wild cheers from the audience, for the American soldier at full gallop carried Old Glory, waving bravely, around the arena three times.

In the meantime the Chinese soldiers and opium-smoking fiends on top of the wall, seeing the American flag, began signaling for help and throwing up their arms in gestures that plainly showed that they knew the game was up. Their plight was desperate.

Now the music and the sound of horses' hoofs grew louder and louder until the noise was almost deafening. Then through the half light we saw a company of American soldiers crawling forward on their stomachs. The Chinese soldiers on the wall pointed to this advancing company and ran off to change their battle-axes for rifles. They took aim and fired.

Suddenly the music stopped to allow the sound of battle to proceed without competition. The American boys returned the fire from thirty guns that banged away for quite a while. Now and then a Chinese soldier would throw up his arms and fall behind the wall.

"Another one dead!" was heard whispered.

"And there goes another one!"

Suddenly a group of dashing cavalry riders, with another silk American flag, rode into the arena and three times around before they dismounted and marched boldly to the base of the wall, which they began climbing.

But one could see that this was not an easy task. And our soldiers were finally forced to stand like acrobats on one another's shoulders, making pyramids.

At last, after a long struggle and much shooting, a single man bearing the American flag reached the top of the wall. But an enemy shot laid him low. The flag was about to fall when another one of our brave men, with a superhuman effort, clambered to the top, caught the flag, and waved it aloft.

The house went wild.

With the flag waving on top of the wall, new courage came to our American troops. Now a dozen or more men scaled the wall. Some stopped to kill the Chinese soldiers in yellow silk coats; others jumped down behind the wall and unbolted the heavy doors of the gate.

As the doors opened the band struck up the American anthem. Now companies of English, French, and Japanese soldiers, each with its proper flag, entered the arena, to march twice around and through the open gate over which waved the American flag.

We were hoarse from cheering and exhausted by the pain and glory of the whole business. But we went home satisfied, for now we knew exactly how the Boxer Rebellion had taken place and how the American boys had discharged their duty in the far Orient.

Secretly I had hoped to catch a glimpse of the Dowager Empress, for this old woman who ruled so many hundreds of millions of people had stirred my imagination. But she did not appear on the wall of Peking during the Rebellion. And I concluded that this was just as it should be, for no woman would ever get into so dangerous a position, especially an Empress. And if Queen Victoria did not go to the war in South Africa, then why should the Chinese Empress get up on the wall of her city in a time like this?

So vividly was the Boxer Rebellion enacted by Buffalo Bill's Wild West Show that no history book has ever been able to persuade me that the details of this battle were otherwise. The way I saw it that night is the way it must certainly have happened.

The Boxer Rebellion and the Buffalo Bill Show took place in 1900, but something very important had happened before that: an old century ended and a new century began. The year 1899 came to an end, and with the new year, 1900, the Twentieth Century was born. Although some purists claimed that the Nineteenth Century did not officially end until December 31, 1900, we paid no attention and went right ahead with welcoming the new century on the first day of 1900.

The new century, however, was not to be born without pain. In fact, there were many who said that it would never be born at all. This was a worrying thought. I was nine years old and just getting a good grip on things. And now along came some ministers and astrologers who were certain that the world would end. It had to end, they said, because the world was so sinful. No one, they predicted, would ever see the dawn of 1900. And so all our heroic efforts in the wide-flung places of the globe were for naught. Before New Year's Day everything would be over! The ministers had clear proof of this coming disaster. From the Bible they quoted lines the meaning of which was unmistakable. And the astrologers said that the stars in the sky bore out the same conclusion.

But while both were agreed on the coming calamity, there was a difference of opinion as to the method. Some of these peddlers of doom said that the end would come by fire, others thought it would come by flood. Still others, a special group of stargazers, chose a more interesting method. They said that the world would suddenly get off the track of its orbit and crash into the sun or else just drop off into space, burning gaily like a meteor.

All these accounts were printed in the daily papers. There were a lot of headlines and a lot of talk. The entire city took sides. And I was scared. When I heard people talk about the end of the world my ears tingled and my eyes grew large. I believed everything I heard. People spoke so earnestly! and I was sure that sincerity meant truth. It was such a serious business and so terrible to think about! Here I was, so young, and I had to die. And the worst of it all was that everyone would have to die without glory. Against the end of the world there was nothing that one could do.

Now, there were others in New York who felt the way I did. They did not want to die either. So they devised a plan whereby a compromise would be effected with fate. I read this note of hope in the papers. These people were sure that, although the new century would be ushered in by a disaster, still it would not be a complete disaster. The world would survive, only it would be taught a good lesson. Either a tidal wave or a great explosion would take place, and many would lose their lives, but some would survive and see the dawn of the new century.

There were still others who, like Grandpa, did not believe a word of it all. But they had the weaker side of the argument. They were contradicting the Bible and they overlooked the heavenly constellations. No matter, then, how much Grandfather tried to comfort me and explain to me why the world would not come to an end, it was hard for me to believe that he could be right and all the others wrong.

I wrote the number 1900 on a piece of paper, just to see how it would look. And it did look strange—so strange that I thought surely Grandpa was mistaken.

Besides, I knew that such things had happened before. I knew this because Dr. Kieran had read to us many stories from the Bible of floods, plagues, fire and brimstone. And with sorrow and fear locked inside me I waited as day by day we came closer and closer to calamity.

As the fateful day drew near we read in the newspapers of people who had drawn out their money from savings banks and were living like kings. They wanted to enjoy their last days on earth. Even some of those who came into the cigar store were making preparations. A fireman bought a whole handful of good ten-cent cigars. These, he said, were for his comfort during the disaster. Another man bought a whole boxful, which he said he would distribute at the proper time.

And when Mrs. O'Leary came in she said: "There's no doubt about it, the world is full of sin. And if the Lord should see fit to punish us all, I'll not be surprised. It's too bad that the good will have to suffer with the bad. If I can get my man sobered we'll say a prayer together." With these words she took a healthy pinch of snuff, which brought on an explosive sneeze.

"God bless you," said my grandfather.

"Bless us all," she said. "I must get my man sobered up. It would be a terrible thing to have a calamity and he not even know it."

But Schultz, the fiddle maker, was on Grandpa's side. He said: "Ach! Vat never vas vill never be."

And Mr. Quaff, the actor, said: "If the world is to end, then it will be the greatest final curtain ever. But we will all be together and on the same stage. For is not all the world a stage? And are not all the men and women merely players?" However, this idea of everyone being an actor and our all being together was little comfort to me.

Finally the last day of the old year arrived. And so far nothing had happened. But there were still some hours to live through before midnight. And who could tell?

That evening after supper Grandpa proposed that we all go to Broadway to see the new century in. I thought this was risky, but, not wanting to stay home alone, I went along.

As we came closer to Broadway the streets became more and more crowded with people. And I was struck by their boldness. Either they had not read the papers or else they were just defiant. The restaurants and hotels that we passed were filled with people having a good time. They wore fancy paper hats and drank champagne.

Out on the street the crowds were blowing horns and rattling tin cans. Everyone was gay and boisterous. Boys tooted horns in the ears of passing girls. And the girls giggled and laughed and ran away.

When we finally reached Broadway it was close to midnight. We watched the hands of a large clock on one of the big buildings as they came closer and closer to midnight. I waited breathlessly. Any second now something might happen!

At last the fateful moment was reached. The hands of the clock joined together, indicating midnight—a new year—a new century.

Church bells began to toll, and the steam whistles of the river boats, small and large, piping and low-moaning, all let loose at one time. We on the streets blew tin horns until our breath was gone. And some beat on pans while others jangled cowbells. Never before had I known an old year to end with such a racket. Never before had a new year come in with such joy.

I got home tired and sleepy and, oh! so happy that the world had not come to an end. Now I could go on living. Now I would see a new century.

2

The New Century

*T*HE PEDDLERS OF DOOM WERE NOT really wrong. The old world had come to an end on New Year's Eve, even though there was no fire or flood. And the next morning, January first 1900, with the beginning of the new century, a new world was born.

During the first years of this new century our lives were to be completely changed. We were to see the development of electricity and of the automobile, the birth of the airplane and of the motion picture, dramatic advances in medicine and the expansion of democracy through the rise of the working class. All these new things were to come into our lives and cause a great upheaval. The changes were to be so rapid that what occurred might even be called a revolution.

But when the city awoke on that first day of 1900 nobody seemed to be aware of what was to come, not even our newspapers. Everything went on the same as always. The newspapers continued manufacturing news and recording events after they had happened. They, too, lacked the vision to see what was to come, even though the changes cast long shadows before us all.

I think that Grandpa, Grandma, and I were some of the first people in New York to become aware of the new world,

73

because when I woke up on that very first day of the Twentieth Century I did not feel so well. And two days later I was sick in bed, and science came right into our home.

When Grandmother saw that I had a very bad sore throat and a high fever she was terribly upset. She sent for Dr. Lambert and for my mother right away. And they didn't waste any time in coming. Grandma and my mother stood beside the bed while Dr. Lambert examined my throat. They didn't say anything, but I knew they were very upset. And when Dr. Lambert said "Diphtheria" they looked at each other and then at Dr. Lambert, and I knew what they were thinking.

Diphtheria was one of the most dreaded of all childhood diseases. With diphtheria the throat often became so inflamed that it closed completely. When this happened the doctor had to open the windpipe and insert a tube so that the child could continue breathing. But even with this operation many children did not survive, because the toxin of the illness was so violent. Against the effect of the toxin there was nothing that could be done, and when the city was swept by an epidemic hundreds of children would die as their parents and doctors stood by helplessly.

Dr. Lambert naturally sensed how upset Mother and Grandmother were, and he tried to comfort them. "Don't worry," he said. "He'll be all right. I'm going to try something new. It's a medicine derived from horse's blood which has been used with success. I'm going to try it."

"Pills?" asked my grandmother anxiously.

"No, it's a serum that we inject—an antitoxin. I have to

go to the Board of Health station to get it, but I'll come right back."

By the time Dr. Lambert returned I was delirious, and I do not remember the injection. But several hours later my fever went down, and that night when Dr. Lambert came to see how things were I was a great deal better.

"It's a miracle," said Mother. "It's a miracle," agreed Grandma.

And it really was a miracle. From that time on antitoxin was widely used, and diphtheria, which had once killed so many children, was no longer the dreaded disease it had been.

There were many parents who refused to allow the doctors to administer antitoxin to their children. They said that it was not natural and that it was poisonous. They maintained that human blood should never be polluted with foreign substances. God, they said, did not approve.

But it did not take long before the public saw that the children who received antitoxin lived, and that many of those who were not injected died. And so the objections became fewer and fewer. And the poison theory collapsed.

But the Angel of Death, who in those days hovered over us constantly, had at his disposal other diseases besides diphtheria. Every day we heard of someone in the neighborhood who had died of either pneumonia, tuberculosis, scarlet fever, typhoid, smallpox, or any one of a dozen other diseases. And operations of any sort were considered a passport to another world. Infant mortality was very high, and on almost every street there was a sign, "Midwife."

Everywhere one went in those days one saw people suffering from tuberculosis. They walked about flushed with fever, thin, weak, and coughing. Every tenement in the city had at least one man, woman, or child who was coughing his life away. Very often whole families were dying. Even the rich were not immune. And each year thousands of people died of this illness.

Smallpox was still prevalent in spite of vaccination. People were careless and did not take advantage of ready immunity, and people with pock-marked faces were commonly seen on the streets. One also saw many people with red eyelids, skin eruptions, open sores, and decayed teeth. It was a usual sight to see people with handkerchiefs tied around their heads. This meant a toothache.

One also saw people crippled by rheumatism. And we heard a great deal about gout, house-maid's knee, and corns and bunions. People were forever saying, with expressions of great pain on their faces: "He stepped right on my corn!" or "My corns are twitching. It's a sure sign of rain."

We had still one more illness to fear, a hangover from Biblical times: leprosy. Leprosy fired our imaginations, and the city simmered with rumors about this disease. Most of the rumors were false. But that did not make any difference, because they were all so believable.

First of all, we believed that leprosy was highly contagious and that anyone discovered to have it was at once removed to a special place. We had all heard that there was a leper house on an island in the East River. The prospect of landing in this place was not a cheerful one. Those who entered never returned. Another rumor widely circulated was that the Chinese in our city were infected with this disease.

This false charge against a helpless minority group caused them much unhappiness. They were looked upon with as much suspicion as if the charge had been true.

One man's sorrow is often another's man's fortune, and so it was in this case. The white people who ran laundries in New York took advantage of the scare, got together, and had posters printed to display in their windows. These posters gave photographic proof of the horrors of leprosy. And under the pictures was printed in bold type: "Do not patronize Chinese laundries. This may happen to you!" Fear and ignorance made us believe the lie.

Yes, in those days the Angel of Death was a very real figure. But year by year, as the new century slowly began to unfold, the shadow of his wings grew less and less. Each year science and medicine added to the well-being and health of the people. As the years went by, the dread of many diseases diminished, and the difference was reflected in the city streets. One no longer saw great numbers of people disfigured by disease. Such sights became rare.

During the days that I spent in bed recovering from diphtheria something secret was going on downstairs in the cigar store. Grandma and Grandpa would not tell me what it was. But I was sure that it had something to do with the new century. And I was right.

At last I was allowed out of bed, and the first thing I did was to hurry downstairs. And there it was! I had guessed it. There was the new century, bright as day, right in Grandpa's cigar store.

Never before had I seen a place so bright and gay. It was

dazzling. It was brighter than the electricity they had downtown. Grandpa had installed gas mantles!

The cigar store had formerly been lighted by ordinary gas jets. But now, added to the old fixtures, there were these modern mantles with glass globes. They were cone-shaped filaments, and they gave off a brilliant light, a light so strong that one could hardly look at it. Science was truly wonderful.

Grandma and Grandpa stood and watched me. They smiled. "Do you like it?" asked Grandpa.

"You bet I do. Of course I do. It is all as bright as sunshine. I can see everything."

"Are you sure you see everything?"

I wondered what Grandpa meant and quickly looked about. There were the snuff jars, there was the happy Negro boy, and there— There was a telephone!

It was the most beautiful telephone in the whole world. And it stood in our store. It was our telephone, all ours.

Of course I had seen telephones before. They had them downtown in the newspaper offices, and there was one in the drugstore a few blocks away. But I had never before seen one in a cigar store. And I could not think of anything more wonderful.

I went over and examined it very carefully. The whole machine was built into a carved mahogany table. The receiver hung on a hook at the side with a small crank close by. And the transmitter into which one spoke was attached to an iron swan's neck that rose gracefully from the center of the table top. In the rear, lying across the length of the table, there was a long, narrow box that contained all the electrical apparatus. Through the glass panel that formed the front of this box you could see silver bells, magnets, coils, and endless wires wound in brilliant green silk.

It was truly beautiful.

Early that spring, as a reward for having been a good boy when I was sick with diphtheria, Grandpa took me to the bicycle show at Madison Square Garden.

In those days bicycles were in vogue. Hundreds of men, women, and children rode through the streets. In fact, there were so many bicycle riders in New York that on Sundays and holidays certain city streets were reserved for the riders, and in Central Park and on Riverside Drive there were special bicycle lanes.

Like most boys I dreamed of some day owning a bicycle. And when Grandpa and I went to the bicycle show I inspected every make with the critical eye of a future buyer. This was no easy task, for there were hundreds and hundreds of bicycles on exhibition. There were not only single-seaters, but also tandems and bicycles with three and even more saddles. Then there were all kinds of displays of bicycle accessories: bells, saddles, fancy handle bars and grips, special pedals, and leather tool cases with screwdrivers, monkey wrenches, oilcans, and sticks of graphite to lubricate the chains. There were also displays of different makes of tires and lamps. Some of the lamps used kerosene, and others burnt acetylene gas.

Everything that I saw at the bicycle show seemed wonderful. Everything was so new and shiny, so enameled and nickel-plated! It was truly a bicycle heaven.

But as Grandpa and I wandered from one booth to the

next examining and admiring, I became more and more confused. Was a chain drive better than a gear drive? Would a
blue bicycle look better than a black one? And what kind
of lamp should I buy? With so much to choose from it was
difficult to make up one's mind. But suddenly everything was
settled for me, and my dream of owning a bicycle faded
away so rapidly that I never really knew where it went.
There, right in the middle of the hall, on a raised platform,
decorated with red, white, and blue bunting, stood an automobile!

I had heard and read about horseless carriages, but I had
never seen one before. And now, here right before me, stood
the finest thing I had ever seen.

It was really fine, but rather curious. It was a cross between a buckboard carriage and a bicycle. It had the body,
upholstered seat, and springs of a carriage, but the wheels
were made of thin metal spokes with rubber tires, just like
a bicycle's. The steering rod was a piece of bent bicycle tub-
ing with a rubber grip from a handle bar. And the wheels
were engaged like a bicycle's with sprockets and chains. Yet
the brass lamps on the front were from a carriage! All in all
it looked very strange, but it was very fascinating, too, especially when one realized that under the seat was hidden a
one-cylinder gas engine capable of moving the whole thing
forward at the rate of ten miles an hour.

Grandpa and I examined this horseless carriage from every
possible angle. It had lots of polished brass, and it was
started by a hand crank. I decided that this was the real
thing. And secretly I made up my mind that from now on
I would save my pennies to buy one.

It was strange, but within the same week I saw another horseless carriage. This time it came puffing and smoking down the street, making a terrible racket. Everyone stopped and stared. Then we all burst out laughing. It was such a funny sight, and the man who was driving it looked so scared! And some of the people on the street yelled "Get a horse! Get a horse!"

Very soon after this I saw still another horseless carriage. In fact, within the next six months I saw four of them. They were breaking out like measles. Now each day the papers printed stories about automobiles, and it was not long before magazines started printing the advertisements of rival manufacturers.

I read everything I could about these new machines. It was interesting to know that five years before the turn of the century there had been just four horseless carriages in the United States, whereas by 1900 there were already eight thousand. Ten years later 200,000 cars were manufactured in a single year, and over two hundred companies contributed to this output.

In the very early days most of the cars were one-cylinder affairs that generated about seven horsepower. The Oldsmobile, one-cylinder model, sold for $650. But later there was a four-cylinder Oldsmobile that generated twenty-eight horsepower and sold for $2,500. With twenty-eight horsepower it was able to do twenty to twenty-five miles an hour!

Cadillacs and Studebakers were also being manufactured, and they cost between three and five thousand dollars without speedometers and lamps. These were sold as extra equipment.

There was also a car called the Northern which was widely advertised as "the only car which is dustless on the road." I could not figure out why this should be so, but since I never saw a Northern I cannot say that this claim was not true.

Mechanically the bicycle is a simple machine, which any boy can understand. But an automobile is quite a different thing. And we boys studied very hard. We had found a new passion. We were auto crazy. Many boys, like me, sent away ten cents in stamps to auto companies for printed sheets and skeleton diagrams showing the working parts of cars. We studied these sheets and catalogues together and argued the merits of one make against another. We spoke about chain drive, gear drive, magnetos, carburetors, compression, and advanced spark. We were completely absorbed in the subject. And whenever we chanced to see a car parked on the street we inspected it from head to tail and noted everything new or different. And should a car be broken down or stalled, as many were in those days, then whole groups of men and boys gathered about to watch it being repaired. There was a fascination about automobiles that was irresistible.

The automobile rushed into American life with a great puffing and smoking. It frightened horses and lots of people who thought it was sure to explode. It was ridiculed and laughed at. But that did not matter. The automobile went on multiplying year after year. It even brought new words into our language, most of them French. We were all soon freely speaking of chauffeurs, garages, coupés, chassis, carburetors, and rubber tires that were pneumatic. The very word automobile was French. And these words became part of our living language.

With the start of the new century the automobile rushed into American life determined to stay. In a very few years it was completely accepted; in a very few years we could hardly remember what life had been like without it.

Several months after the bicycle show I saw my first movie.

The hot weather of early summer had come, and one Sunday Grandpa and I went to Coney Island to bathe in the sea. It was here, in a saloon, that Grandpa and I saw a movie.

Now if Grandma had been with us, we should have missed it all, for she was against liquor in any form. Well, not in all forms. We did have a cut-glass decanter of blackberry brandy on the sideboard, but this was reserved for serious stomach-aches. As a family we must have had strong digestions, for in all the years of my youth the level of the blackberry brandy dropped only one inch.

There was no question about it, Grandma was dead set against liquor, and if she had been with us we should never have entered that saloon. In fact, her influence over Grandpa was so great that I had trouble getting him past the door. But I must have been persuasive, and the lure of the motion picture proved irresistible.

It all happened this way:

As we were walking along one of the streets I noticed some boys crouched low to the ground, peering under a loose canvas that covered the entrance of a café. I could hear the tinkle of a piano and roars of laughter. Surely something was going on; I had to investigate. I crouched down low beside the boys and peeked under the canvas.

Inside all was in semidarkness. Men and women sat at small round tables drinking beer. And on the far wall, on a white sheet hanging from the ceiling, I saw something I had never seen before. It was good. And from this first moment I was a captive.

There on the sheet was a picture of people in a room, and they were moving about just as in real life. True, their motions were quick and jerky, but I did not care, because they were doing such funny things. They were hitting each other over the head with bottles and mallets. And a little man was trying to escape the fury of a big man, while a woman in a plumed hat stood by crying and wringing her hands in anguish. Then a policeman came, and he too joined in the battle. It was wonderful, and so terribly funny! But just when the excitement was the greatest someone grabbed my arm and pulled me away. It was Grandpa.

"Come along," he said.

"Oh, oh, Grandpa. You didn't see what it was. It's a picture, and it's funny. Let's go in."

"What's funny about a picture?"

Just then a rolling roar of laughter came from the café.

"See, Grandpa, it's funny. It's like a magic lantern, only everyone moves. And they are breaking bottles over each other's heads. It's all on a bed sheet hanging from the ceiling."

Grandpa was immediately interested. A picture that moved, a bed sheet, people being hit over the head—

"Come on, let's go in," I pleaded.

I could see that Grandpa was willing, but that something was holding him back. Suddenly I realized what it was—Grandma. "How can we go in?" asked Grandpa. "It's a saloon."

"But they have pictures in there, and everyone is laughing!"

I was disappointed. But I understood. Liquor was a very sinful thing, and it would not be right for us to go into a saloon. What would Grandma ever think?

We stood there in front of the loose flapping canvas and we heard the people laughing inside. We could not go in, and still we did not go away. We just stood there on the sidewalk side by side in silence.

Suddenly another roar of laughter came from the café. That settled everything.

"A light glass of beer never made anyone drunk," said Grandpa, taking me by the arm and opening the canvas flap. In another moment we were inside sitting at a little round table, and Grandpa was ordering a glass of beer.

We saw the picture from beginning to end. And when it was finished we saw it all over again. We saw it twice, and then we were satisfied. We knew every blow that was struck, every attack and every escape.

And as we left the saloon my Grandfather said: "It's very good. But I don't think that it should be encouraged, because it's just an invention to sell more beer."

However, Grandpa was wrong. Within the next few years the flickering drama came out of the saloons and into empty stores all over the city. These stores were equipped with folding chairs rented from undertakers. And people came just to see the picture and have a good time. No beer was served. Everyone paid a nickel to enter. And it was not long before these little motion picture shops were known as nickelodeons.

Grandma, Grandpa, and I went often to the neighborhood nickelodeon. In fact, everyone went. They were very popular. And I must say that month by month the pictures improved. They grew longer, the chases more exciting, the heroines more helpless. And to the bottles and mallets were added custard pies.

Besides the movies the new century brought us still another source of amusement: Suffragettes.

Suffragettes were women who thought that it was only just and reasonable for women to have equal political rights with men. Through the years American women had slowly managed to enter industry, business, and the professions. It had been a long, slow climb, but in time they had made their way into man's world. Now only the vote was still denied them.

In a few western states and territories women had already been granted the vote. But in the East the prevailing sentiment was against it. Here the struggle between men and women, and between women and women, went on year after year. Almost all men and most women thought that woman suffrage was absurd. The upper classes ridiculed it. The poor of the lower classes were dead set against it. And even the vast majority of the middle class could see little justice in the idea. Yet from each class there were a few, a very few, who were willing to fight for women's rights.

These women banded together. They joined the suffragette movement that had started over fifty years before. They took every opportunity to bring their cause forward. In fact, they were something of a nuisance. They were everywhere, picketing, distributing leaflets, and petitioning. They held meetings, they spoke on street corners.

I often listened to them. And it seemed to me that their reasoning was clear and logical. But the crowds that gathered about them booed and jeered and threw out insults. And strangely enough it was the women in the crowds who did most of the booing.

Everyone seemed set against the suffragettes. Politicians said that women belonged in the home. Ministers branded woman's suffrage as immoral. They said that if women got the vote they would neglect their children and bring ruin to the American home.

But against this swamping tide of opposition the suffragettes fought on. They were determined. And each year, just to bring their cause to the attention of the public, they paraded down Fifth Avenue. This parade was a sight to see, and it attracted a huge crowd, just as hostile as it was big. The determined leaders of the suffragettes led the parade riding on great white work horses rented from a livery stable. They rode sidesaddle and wore costumes of flowing capes and plumed hats. Behind them came lines of women marchers carrying lots of banners, signs, and American flags. But the best part of the parade was always at the end. Here there was a small contingent of frightened men—husbands, brothers, sons, and friends pressed into service.

As the parade came down the Avenue the crowds that

lined the streets laughed and booed and threw some spe-
cially selected eggs and vegetables at the marchers. The suffragettes did not mind. Their cause was a noble one, and
such attacks were to be expected in the war they were wag-
ing. But the frightened company of men, not bolstered by
the spirit of the noble cause, did not enjoy the sudden shower
of eggs and vegetables. And it often happened that some lost
their nerve and were driven from the ranks.

When they took to their heels and ran, the crowds went
wild.

While some women were fighting for the right to vote,
other women were busy defending their modesty. They felt
that electricity was rudely invading their privacy.

In Europe a scientist by the name of Roentgen had in-
vented the X-ray machine, and now that a few of these machines had come to America the air was filled with rumors.
Everyone had seen pictures printed in the papers of bones
photographed by X-ray, and it was therefore known that
these rays could penetrate. The rumor spread that anyone
owning one of these machines, a scheming scientist or evil
doctor, could sit at his window and, by turning on the current, look through the clothing of people passing in the
street. This was of course dreadful. And women especially
had to be protected.

Every fireman and policeman who came into our store
agreed that something should be done.

"Science has gone too far," said one.

"This whole invention should be destroyed," said another.

"It's not decent," added a third. "The public must be protected."

An enterprising corset maker came to the rescue. He would protect American womanhood! He advertised and manufactured an X-ray-proof corset. It was guaranteed to block any rays that one might happen to run into while walking down the street.

With the beginning of the new century, electricity truly came into our lives. I had for many years seen electric lights downtown, but now electric lights were being installed uptown in many buildings and homes. And although most of our city streets were still lit by gaslight, and the lamplighters made their rounds every evening at dusk, there were now some important avenues that had hissing arc lamps.

Many of our streetcars were being run by electrical motors, and the elevated steam trains were also being converted. They were even building an underground railway, a subway. With electricity it was also possible for elevators to go up many stories in a building, and in 1902 the first skyscraper was built in New York City. And my mother had her law office in this skyscraper—the Flatiron Building on Twenty-third Street and Fifth Avenue.

It seemed as though, overnight, our city was changing its ways. It was being electrified. Even the wonderful steam trains on Park Avenue were now being replaced by electrical engines.

From this moment on there was no more steam or soot, and Park Avenue became much too clean for the poor. The old wooden bridges were torn down, the railroad cut covered over, and a fine avenue came into being. Now the factories and tenements disappeared and were replaced by big hotels and apartment houses. The rich moved in.

It was about this time—December 1901—that Marconi sent his first wireless message across the Atlantic. Such a thing was almost beyond man's imagination. The news that a message could travel thousands of miles through the air without wires was sensational. Our newspapers printed many stories about Marconi and his experiments, and everyone in New York spoke of this new wonder. There were many who felt that wireless would prove of little use because we already had an Atlantic cable; but very soon after this first message was sent across the Atlantic, wireless apparatus was installed on some large ocean liners. Through wireless and Morse code these ships were able at all times to communicate with land and with each other. Now people began to realize that Marconi's wireless was really important.

X-ray, railroad electrification, and wireless were big electrical things and out of the reach of the ordinary boy. There were, however, small electrical things that every boy could have. There were batteries, wet and dry; there were miniature electrical motors; and there were push-button bells. And I had one of each.

I spent hours and hours experimenting. I liked the push-button bell the best, and I could adjust the make and break to give its ring a different tone. I could make lots of sparks one after another and smell the ozone, and I could stretch the wires all over the apartment and, standing in a far bedroom, make the bell ring in the living room under the couch. Then, disconnecting the bell, I could put the two wires from the battery to my tongue and taste the salty tingle of electricity.

It was a long time before I exhausted all the possibilities of my electric bell, and then I turned to my electric motor. It could run on one battery, but with two it would spin like mad. However, it was so small that its uses were limited, and I had trouble finding things for it to do.

While boys were playing with motors and bells adults were buying electrical vibrators to cure gout and rheumatism. These machines, run on batteries, had two metal handles, and these the hopeful patient gripped, thus allowing the healing current to pass through his body.

Reinhardt and I had access to one of these machines, which belonged to his grandfather. Sometimes when no one was around we took a treatment. It was very nice to have the sensation of pins and needles tingling through you. But once while I was holding the handles Reinhardt accidentally turned the current on so high that I could not let go. I just stood and shook. I could not even call out. Reinhardt thought I was enjoying it; he stood by and talked. But after a while, when I did not answer him, he sensed that something was wrong and pulled the switch.

That I have never developed gout or rheumatism I attribute to this near electrocution.

While vibrators were being sold to cure gout and rheumatism there were simpler devices with other virtues. One could buy belts charged with static electricity that were particularly good for abdominal difficulties. One could also buy inner soles for one's shoes. These inner soles had a row of small copper and zinc disks down the middle which were supposed to generate a mild current as one walked. They were designed to give one zest and vitality where it was most needed, on the soles of the feet.

Electricity was changing our city and our lives, but it did not occupy all our time. We boys had other things to think about; things that were just as much fun, like flying kites.

On good breezy days we often hurried over to Central Park, where the wide green lawns gave us plenty of room to run and launch our kites. It was all good fun and very cheap. You could buy a kite in a candy shop for two pennies; then, with a ten-cent ball of cord and some old rags for a tail, you could send it high into the sky. We spent hours and hours flying kites. We held contests to see whose kite would go the highest. And some boys made their own kites, very large and painted in bright colors.

One day a boy came into the park with a new kind of kite. All of us gathered around him and asked him lots of questions. His kite was made of sticks and cloth and was called a box kite. It did really resemble a hollow box, and we thought it looked most curious. But it went up easily and flew steadily without a tail. It climbed and climbed and floated about high in the air. We on the ground watched it. And the boy let us hold the cord to feel the pull.

"Gee, it's strong," said one.

"It will break the cord," added another.

"The pull is so strong," said a third, "that if it were bigger I bet it could lift a boy right off the ground and fly away with him."

The idea of being lifted off the ground by a kite appealed

to us. This would be a new kind of adventure. And all afternoon we discussed this possibility.

In the months that followed, many boys bought box kites, even though they were expensive and sold for fifty cents, seventy-five cents, and a dollar, according to size. And whenever a box kite was flown a discussion would arise. In fact it was always the same discussion: How big would a box kite have to be to raise a boy off the ground? Some said that if it were ten times as large as the largest kite now made, then it would surely raise up a hundred-pound boy. Others said no, the whole idea was foolish.

This argument went on all season, and we had almost exhausted it when one day, to our surprise, there appeared in the newspapers a picture of a glider that resembled a large box kite. This glider, it was reported, had lifted a man off the ground!

And it was not long after this that the newspapers ran a story about two bicycle mechanics in Ohio, brothers by the name of Wright, who were planning to build a glider with a gas engine and two propellers. They had the idea that the engine and propellers would keep their glider flying through the air.

We boys liked the idea, but all the grownups seemed to be of the opinion that this was going a bit too far and that the two brothers in Ohio must be a little touched in the head. Everyone could, of course, understand why a balloon filled with gas could raise in the air. Here a reasonable principle was involved. But how could anyone believe that a machine heavier than air could be made to fly?

Mrs. O'Leary said: "There will be plenty of time for flying

when we pass through the Golden Gates and St. Peter gives us our wings. Mark me words, the whole thing's unnatural and no good will come of it."

And Schultz, the fiddle maker, laughed. He thought it was funny for men to want to sail through the air. "If you want to fly I'll tell you how. Go up on the roof, open an umbrella, and jump off. That's how to fly." He laughed so hard that he held his sides. He thought it a good joke.

And there were others besides Mrs. O'Leary and Mr. Schultz who were against the idea of flying. In fact, I do not remember hearing one voice raised in defense of the Wright brothers. Everyone laughed or criticized.

Professor Simon Newcomb, a noted scientist, wrote an article for a magazine in which he proved conclusively by mathematics and logic that it was impossible for men to fly. He said that it was nonsense to try, for even if man were able to rise from the ground, once he slackened his speed down he would fall like a stone. What Professor Newcomb said was supported by Admiral George W. Melville, Chief Engineer of the U.S. Navy, in an article in the *North American Review*. In this article he explained convincingly the absurdity of man's attempts to fly.

These experts only confirmed what the public felt. And some time later when the newspapers reported that the two bicycle mechanics in Ohio had failed a dozen times to raise their machine from the ground, everyone was satisfied.

But one day in the middle of the winter of 1903 we were much surprised when we picked up our newspapers to read that the same two persistent brothers had finally got their machine to fly. It seemed that the Wright brothers had launched their machine on the sandy beach of Kittyhawk, North Carolina. They had chosen this particular beach because here there was always a good breeze, which they felt was necessary. They had run their machine down a single track to give it impetus, and on the very first trial it had risen on the breeze and actually stayed in the air for twelve seconds. They tried again and again, and on the fourth trial it had remained in the air for fifty-nine seconds and had covered a distance of 852 feet.

This epoch-making event, which was to change the future of the whole world, was witnessed by a mere handful of curious people from the neighborhood. And only one local newspaper man was present. Since every newspaper in the country felt that the Kittyhawk trials would just end in failure, they did not see the need to cover the story. And thus the news and details of this important flight did not filter out into the world until some days later.

Even after this, when the impossible had been accomplished, the public still seemed to feel that flying would never amount to anything and that "the Wright brothers were just wasting their time." In spite of their success the Wright brothers were still being ridiculed.

In fact, everything that was new and important in the early 1900's was ridiculed. The more important it was and the more it threatened to change our lives, the more it was laughed at. There was blind resistance to any change.

However, a year after the Kittyhawk flight there was a sudden change in public sentiment. That spring the Wright brothers accomplished another successful flight, this time in Dayton, Ohio.

I do not remember how long their machine stayed in the air, but I know that it stayed long enough for flying to stop being considered a joke. In the public mind it had suddenly become an achievement. And from that moment on, aviation took wings.

The peddlers of doom were not wrong: the old world had died. And a new world had arrived, bringing with it advances in medicine, electricity, automobiles, motion pictures, wireless, and the airplane.

In the years that followed, religion, poetry, music, and art seemed no longer to satisfy man. They seemed no longer to sustain him. The roar of the machine drowned out the voice from the wilderness. And man turned to new hopes—to economics and science. In these he saw a promise of a better life.

There was now a new tempo. We entered the modern world.

3

Spring and Summer

*E*ACH YEAR SPRING CAME TO NEW York with St. Patrick's Day. And, even though the March weather might still be blustery and bleak, the celebrations of the Irish on this day warmed the air so thoroughly that nature could no longer resist. Everyone who lived in New York knew this, and all of us looked forward to St. Patrick's Day, even though most of us were not Irish. We also looked forward to a wonderful parade and gay celebrations.

Things got started early on St. Patrick's Day. Vendors came through the streets with green ribbons, dyed carnations, little pots of shamrock, and celluloid buttons with pictures of green harps. They sold these souvenirs easily and quickly. Not only did the Irish buy them, but others too, in honor of the good saint, adorned themselves with a touch of green.

However, it was the Irish who really understood the meaning of "the wearing of the green." On this day they suddenly appeared in green hats, shirtwaists, and ties; green coats, trousers, gloves, and scarfs. Everything was bright green.

The parade was held on Fifth Avenue early in the afternoon, and all of New York that was not marching came out to line the way. And it was always a sight worth seeing. Here before our eyes paraded the Hibernian slice of New York: beautiful colleens, plump matrons with fine complexions, politicians, saloonkeepers, contractors, labor leaders, and workmen, old men with clay pipes and happy boys and girls from parochial schools. All the Irish were on the march. There were so many of them that it made a very long parade. And it was always lively and colorful. There were many bands and drum corps, bagpipes and harps. There were lots of banners and shillelaghs. And in every parade there was at least one big sign that read "England, Get Out of Ireland!"

The rank and file walked, but all the important Irishmen in New York, to mark their superiority, rode on horses. They wore Prince Alberts, striped trousers, high silk hats, and bright green sashes. On this day there suddenly appeared so many important Irishmen that there were not enough saddle horses in the city to go around, and so a great number were forced to ride on heavy draught horses rented from livery stables. But this did not matter. The spirit of St. Patrick was a happy one, and conventions were cast aside.

Preparations for the parade began in the early morning. The long march started at noon. And in the late afternoon many of the marchers were still marching, but this time up Third Avenue, where they could stop at each corner to refresh themselves. By sundown it seemed that every Irishman in the city was on Third Avenue.

But happiness did not come to them quickly. It took many stations, many songs, and many jigs. In time, however, one could sense a mounting joy.

I was very fortunate in having a ringside seat at the Third Avenue celebrations on St. Patrick's Day. Our cigar store was unusually well located. It overlooked two important saloons, one called Hennessy's and the other, diagonally across the avenue, called O'Toole's.

Now Hennessy's was frequented by Dublin boys and O'Toole's by South Ireland bucks of the sod. But though the Dublin boys felt themselves a bit superior, it made no difference; they were all Irishmen and friends. And all year long they lived in peace with one another. However, too much peace can be a dreary thing. And each year, on St. Patrick's Day, a war broke out between the clienteles of Hennessy's and O'Toole's.

But if you think it is easy to start a war between sons of Ireland who all year have lived in peace, you are very wrong. It is a difficult affair and has to be delicately managed and skillfully brewed. The main ingredients are time and liquor.

As the hours passed in each saloon the men began to think back on other St. Patrick's Days and on the abuses they had suffered from the men of the rival saloon. Their brooding over these injustices gave birth to a spirit of revenge. And in time, from the ranks of each saloon there arose a leader, one who could inspire the men with easy talk and embroidered facts. And he did inspire them. As time passed and liquor flowed he instilled into them a loyalty to each other and an animosity to those in the rival saloon. Presently he was confiding to them that the men across the street were surely plotting another war and that an attack was imminent.

It was quickly decided that certain ones should enter the enemy camp, in a friendly way of course, and report back on any suspicious doings. Needless to say, the reports that filtered back were never good. The friendly envoys had always been insulted. And to defend the honor of their respective saloons they gave back as much as they received.

In this polite way things got started. And each side knew that the time had now come to send forth re-enforcements. The biggest and burliest fortresses of brawn were chosen to go forward and face the enemy. These men were accompanied by small spirited companions whose duty it was to report back on the proceedings.

In no time at all wounding insults were being hurled and a rain of sharp barbed curses fell upon each saloon. With these the spirit grew warmer. And the runners crossed the avenue back and forth reporting the effect of every accusation, every oath, every thorn that had found its flesh.

In time these rival runners ran into one another. But only minor clashes occurred. Only a few quick blows were exchanged, for there was still a good deal of drinking to do before a real mass-upon-mass encounter could begin.

But time and liquor took care of everything. The O'Toole men were soon charging the Hennessy Dublin boys with licking the boots of the King of England. This was a deep insult, and a wound was opened. The Hennessy men charged the O'Toole boys with being black-hearted Protestants. " 'Tis a lie!" they cried. But the words had cut like a knife—another wound inflicted.

Once these gashes had been opened it was the duty of the brave insult-hurlers to stick a fork into the open wound and stir it about. Abuse was piled upon insult, fanning the flames of passion until each saloon was a raging furnace. Now all forces consolidated on home ground.

Then with a cry from the leaders, "Are ye sons of Erin or are ye miserable cowards?" the two saloons would empty themselves on to Third Avenue.

Two dense knots of humanity would start staggering across the avenue towards each other. They moved slowly. They moved with caution.

"Here they come!" would cry one of the leaders. "The spawn of hell! Here come the black-livered sons of devils. And not one of 'em is fit to be a-wearing of the green. Here they come!"

"Devils, are we?" would cry the opposing leader. "Right ye are. And each one of us can lick seven of you!" With these final words there was a lunge forward, and the battle was on.

The avenue was not wide enough for the war that followed. The elevated pillars were in the way and prevented mass movements. Thus the fighting settled down to small groups battling each other, small groups conquering each other. But it is not easy to conquer an Irishman, and many of those who fell to the pavement rose to fight again. They fought on barefisted, pounding away, taking lots of punishment, and showing little fatigue. They were unsteady on their feet, but it did not matter.

And always, when the war was at its height, men arrived from other saloons, blocks away, just to join in. The news had somehow spread. These volunteers did not care on which side they fought, nor were they concerned with the cause of the strife. They fought only for the love of fighting. And since they could see that this was not a private fight, but a public one, they felt that they were not intruding.

In time the police wagon would arrive. But it always arrived late, because on St. Patrick's Day the police, most of whom wore the green, considered it bad form to arrest an Irishman. However, the police performed a gracious service; they picked up the wounded and those who had fallen in the fray and were unable to rise and stagger away. They gave them a ride in the wagon and free lodging overnight in the police station. It was little enough to do for countrymen who had been set upon in the dark by some unknown enemy.

When the war was over and the bodies cleared away, the avenue was always strewn with shattered glass from shop windows and broken Derby hats. And it happened that twice our innocent wooden Indian suffered a broken arm.

I felt very bad about this, but Grandpa said it didn't matter, because we would have it repaired; and besides, since it was now spring, the Indian would have to be repainted anyway.

Each year when St. Patrick's Day announced the arrival of Spring there was a warming of the air and a stirring of the blood. Everyone felt like doing things, especially the housewives. After a long winter they felt that it was time for cleaning; it was time to dust the chandeliers, to wash the curtains, to beat the rugs, to clean out the crowded closets. With the first warm day, then, spring cleaning began. And, oddly enough, a feather duster man emerged as from nowhere. He moved through the streets calling with a birdlike cry: "Feather dusters—all kind." Like a giant bird almost a story tall he moved through the streets. His face and body were completely covered by feather dusters, and some with long handles swayed high above his head.

Those housewives in need of dusters came out and bargained with him. Some needed light ones for their delicate bric-a-brac, others needed stout-handled dusters, and still others needed long-handled ones to reach the fancy plaster work on the ceilings.

On this same first warm day rattrap men also appeared with hundreds of spring traps clamped to their overcoats and bundles of wire cages over their backs. It was also time to clean out the rats! These were followed by the I-cash-clothes men urging everyone to empty their closets, and the clothesline men who called their song from the backyards, "Clotheslines! Clotheslines!" They were ready to climb the tall poles and replace old pulleys and lines that had been damaged by the winter.

With spring the housewives of New York were busy. But there was also another kind of cleaning to be done. The druggists removed their winter window displays of Cod Liver Oil, Mustard Plasters, and Cough Mixtures, and redecorated with Spring Tonics: with Rhubarb, with Beef, Iron and Wine, and with Sulphur and Molasses. In each window there was a sign, "Spring! Time to Clean Your Blood."

As the days grew warmer more vendors wandered through the streets. Where these men had been hibernating all winter no one ever knew, but with the bright clear sun they suddenly appeared. There were the flower men with their wagons gaily filled with geraniums, hyacinths, pansies, and potted palms. There were pot menders, umbrella men, scissors grinders, and window washers. Then when the weather grew really warm the hokeypokey man appeared.

He pushed his little cart down the street until he found a proper place, and then he stopped. The children all gathered around, each with a penny in his hand, and the hokeypokey man went to work. With a scraper he shaved a large block of ice, gathering the snow into a ball on a piece of paper. Then, taking several bottles, filled with colored syrups, he squirted on a little green, some red, some orange. This colored snowball tasted very good, but you had to eat it fast before it melted away! Each vendor had his special cry. It filled the air and came through the open windows with the sunshine. And it was nice to hear.

And there were others who also came with spring. There were hurdy-gurdy men, mournful street singers, and German bands. At the most unexpected moments the beautiful spring air would be filled with strains of "Funiculi, Funicula," "Mother Machree," and "Tannenbaum, O Tannenbaum!" When we heard these tunes we thought of summer and of other music. For with the coming of summer there were band concerts in the city parks.

In Central Park great crowds gathered to listen to the band. And I was usually one of the first to arrive. I liked the music that was played. It was sentimental and descriptive. As I sat there listening I could hear chirping birds, whispering winds, waterfalls, and the march of victorious armies. I liked the "William Tell" and "Poet and Peasant" overtures, and Tchaikovsky's "1812." And I always thought it was nice when they played "The Beautiful Blue Danube."

The band in Central Park was really the best in New

York, but I also listened to an Italian band in Little Italy, a Hungarian band in a park near East Fourth Street, and a German band in Yorkville. There were other bands that played in Harlem and on Riverside Drive. In the summers New York was alive with band music. And the brass of those days had a special timbre and resonance of its own. The musical cadences gave accent to the obvious and the sentimental. But that is how the people like it. This was music everyone could understand.

These band concerts were the only music people could hear free of charge. And everyone came to listen.

At the end of June, as soon as school was closed, we boys began getting ready for the Fourth of July. There wasn't any time to lose, for all together we had less than a week to collect our fireworks and the material for our bonfire.

In those days almost every street in New York had its private bonfire on the Fourth, and Reinhardt and I, together with a lot of other boys from our school, were always determined that our Fifty-second Street fire should be as big and bright as any.

For several days we went about in groups gathering material and storing it in our backyards where we could keep watch over it. We sometimes collected enough stuff to fill a large moving van. Some of the pieces were so heavy that it took a whole gang of us to move them. We collected barrels and wooden boxes from grocers. And we went from house to house consulting with housewives and janitors. Here a lady gave us a bureau, and there we got hold of an old square piano that had lost a leg. At another house we collected two straw mattresses. These we especially prized, they burned so furiously.

We collected old chairs, tables, beds, anything at all that could burn. And we dragged our loot out of cellars and down long flights of stairs, across streets, and into our backyards. We worked hard, and often, as we pushed and pulled some stubborn piece along the sidewalk, people would shake their heads and say: "Some day you boys will burn down the whole block. Then you'll be satisfied."

We never paid any attention to these cranks, but why older people were so afraid of bonfires we could not understand. What could be more exciting? And if our bonfires should get out of hand, the fire engines were always ready. And to see them at work was also a fine sight.

Then there were other people who also tried to spoil our fun. They would stop us on the street and say: "Where are you boys going with that beautiful mahogany bureau?" or "What a shame. Look at that lovely chair!" And if it were a small piece they sometimes tried to take it away from us, but we never surrendered anything. We put up a good fight.

However, when the evening of the Fourth of July arrived we boys did not celebrate alone. Seeing us drag our loot into the center of the street, some of the neighborhood men joined in and helped us. There were always some grownups who understood how to celebrate Independence Day, and they worked just as hard as we did and carried all the heavy pieces themselves. And when the bright flames had consumed most of our stuff they found all kinds of things to feed the bonfire—things that we had no authority to take.

Our Fifty-second Street fire attracted a crowd, for it was

always the biggest and best in the neighborhood. And when it really got going the shower of sparks was beautiful to see. They sometimes rose as high as the buildings.

It was at this moment, when our fire was at its best, that we would shoot off our fireworks. We had lots of Red Devil firecrackers, time bombs, and Roman candles. And it was really good fun when a Roman candle went wild, scattering the crowd or shooting hot balls through open windows!

We always did our very best to celebrate the Fourth in a proper way. And I think everybody in the neighborhood had a good time. That is, almost everybody. There were, of course, a few who did not appreciate our efforts. Some of the home-owners stood on the roofs of their three-story brownstone houses with pails of water ready to put out any sparks that might land. And some others grumbled and said there should be a law—

Once on the day after the Fourth when Mr. Hadley came into the cigar store I heard him say: "These bonfires are getting too big. They will some day burn down the whole city. Last night the fire department had more calls than it could manage. Street fires should be outlawed!" I was truly shocked to hear a good man like Mr. Hadley speak against the spirit of American Independence.

But it really came about as Mr. Hadley had said. Year by year our fires grew bigger, and suddenly one year a city ordinance was passed, and all street fires were forbidden. This of course dampened our spirits. But we still had firecrackers and Roman candles.

Each year as soon as the Fourth of July celebrations were over the people of New York settled in for a good hot summer. They put up awnings to keep the sun off the windows, they fixed up the backyards with tables and chairs, and in the more crowded districts people moved their chairs out on to the sidewalks every evening in order to enjoy the cool air circulating through the streets.

One summer, right after the Fourth, my grandmother said to me: "You and I are going to the country for the rest of the summer."

"Staten Island?" I asked eagerly.

"No," said Grandma. "We're going to the real country, the mountains."

I couldn't understand how country could be more real than Staten Island, but perhaps mountains were different. I had seen pictures of mountains, and they did look wild, much wilder than Staten Island. Grandma was probably right.

At any rate, I liked the whole idea, and I helped Grandma pack a trunk and two suitcases. I had to do this, because there were a lot of things I knew I had to have along, like my battery and bell, my marbles, a screwdriver, a monkey wrench, and my baseball. In time everything was ready. The trunk was sent ahead, and early one morning Grandma and I, carrying our suitcases and a basket of lunch, kissed Mother and Grandpa good-bye and started out.

We took the Third Avenue trolley down to Forty-second Street, where we transferred to the crosstown car that brought us to the Weehawken Ferry House on the west side. The ferry carried us across the river to New Jersey, where

we boarded a West Shore Railroad train. We had already
been traveling for about an hour and a half, and I was getting tired. "How much further do we have to go?" I asked.
"Isn't it going to be country soon?"

But Grandma shook her head. "We've only just started,"
she said. "We've got a long ways to go."

And Grandma was right. Hour after hour our train
puffed and pulled up the west shore of the Hudson River.
And as I looked out of the window all I saw was country,
and country, and more country. I never knew there was so
much country. And I had never dreamed that the Hudson
River was so long.

Occasionally the train stopped at a station in some little
town, but it was all very different from New York, and it
seemed strange to me. After five hours our train arrived at
the Kingston Station, and Grandma said that we were now
a hundred miles north of New York. This was the farthest
I had ever been from my enchanted isle. I was not too sure
I liked it.

Here we changed to another train that brought us into the
wonderful cool green mountains. It puffed along slowly,
winding its way through the valleys and up the mountains,
until we came to a town called Phoenicia. At Phoenicia we
again changed to another train, a spur line that went through
a gap in the mountains to a town called Hunter. It was late
in the afternoon when we reached this place, but we had still
not arrived at our destination. However, Grandma said it
would not take much longer.

At the Hunter Station we were met by a very nice man
with a horse and surrey. He drove us about ten miles farther

over dirt roads, deep into the mountains, close to a place called Jewett Heights. Here we turned off the main road, crossed a rickety old iron bridge that spanned a broad rushing stream, and after climbing a steep hill for almost half a mile came at last to an old white farmhouse perched on the side of the mountain, surrounded by fields, long stone walls, and patches of woodland. This was Persons' Boarding House. This was the place. And after our long journey we were tired and glad to be here.

But even though I was very tired, as we drove into the yard and I looked quickly about I saw all kinds of things that needed my immediate attention. The sun had already set, and my inspection had to be completed before dark. I ran here and there, taking in as much as I could.

I went into the big red barn, which was built on a hillside. It had two large entrances, one below and the other on the high side of the hill, so that wagons could drive in on both levels. In the lower part of the barn I counted fourteen cows. This was an amazing sight. I had never been so close to cows before. In fact, I kept my distance even now, because they looked so strange with their long horns, their big wet noses, and their curling pink tongues. Besides, there was something going on that I didn't quite understand. The farmer and his two sons, each sitting on a stool with a pail between his legs, were getting milk out of the cows in the oddest way ever seen. It came out in sudden squirts and made a funny noise as it went into the pail. I stood and watched for several minutes, but since nobody spoke to me and there were other things to do, I quickly went away.

On the upper level there was a hayloft, and there were

stalls for four beautiful work horses. Behind the barn was a pigpen with a big fat pig and a lot of little ones all sleeping soundly in a mess of mud. As I stood and watched, the big pig opened its eye and looked at me. But it didn't move; it only grunted once or twice.

Nearby there was a chicken house with an open run and lots of big gray hens. They clucked and cackled as I ran past. And next to the henhouse there was an open shed with a buggy and a big mowing machine. I examined it very carefully but couldn't figure out exactly how it worked. But I could see the shaft for the team of horses, the seat for the man, and the levers he had to work.

Close by I came across a long wooden watering trough. We had lots of watering troughs in the city, but none that could water ten horses at one time; besides, ours were made of iron or stone. Then, between the trough and the house was a big garden with rows and rows of green plants. I didn't know what the plants were, but on some vines growing on poles I saw green beans.

Next to the house was a shed filled with neatly stacked firewood. It was close to the kitchen door, and lying before this door was the most beautiful collie dog I had ever seen. I went up and patted him, and he wagged his tail.

A woman came to the door. It was Mrs. Persons. "His name is Rip," she said.

"Rip?" I asked.

"Yes. We named him after Rip Van Winkle, who lived in these mountains."

I had read about Rip Van Winkle and his long sleep, and I was surprised to hear that we were right in the middle of his mountains. And I thought it was a good idea to have named the dog after him.

I petted Rip again. He was a fine dog. And as I petted him I thought that this was a nice farm. I felt that Grandma and I had come to a good place.

There were other boarders, other children, at Persons' Boarding House. And all day long we played together. We ran through the meadows, walked along the top of the stone walls, and climbed trees; we jumped in the hayloft; and we helped Rip bring the cows in from the pasture. We also helped with the haying and rode high on top of the swaying load, across the fields and right into the barn. We rolled rocks down a steep grassy hillside, and when we tired of this we rolled ourselves down the hill.

Sometimes we took long walks through the dark woods, where we saw great moss-covered rocks, ferns, pine cones, and endless other wonders. Overhead we saw the blue sky and the sunlight filtered in millions of bright little spots through the green foliage. It was like a dome of lace.

And each afternoon, with Rip leading the way, we went bathing down in the stream by the rickety old iron bridge. The water was cool and fresh. We dipped and we splashed. And on the way home we always stopped at a special place to visit a very special friend.

Not far from the house, at the edge of a field, was a cold, clear spring that, by gravity feed through hollow logs, supplied water for the farm. And down on the sandy bottom of this spring lived a big speckled trout. Each day we gathered around the edge of the spring and, lifting the old wooden cover, peered down just to make sure that our friend was still there. Occasionally, as we watched, he would come to the surface and snap at a fly!

Here on Persons' farm life was filled with all kinds of adventures and wonderful things. And the most wonderful of all was the way Rip made butter.

Next to the kitchen there was a lean-to used as a dairy. And it was here that twice a week Rip made the butter. He walked a treadmill that turned a flywheel that was connected by a seesaw device with the plunger that splashed up and down in the butter churn. It took a long time to churn the butter, and poor Rip had to walk many treadmill miles before the job was done. He was hot and his tongue hung out. And I felt sorry for him.

The first time I saw Rip in the treadmill, running the churn, my eyes nearly popped out of my head. I had never known how butter was made. And assuming that no one in New York knew, either, I wrote my mother a long letter explaining the whole thing. In the city we bought butter in the dairy stores to which we took our pitchers to be filled with milk. The butter came in tubs, and hunks were cut out with a knife, as many pounds as one needed. But here in the country I learned that butter was made from cream. It was churned!

One day Mr. Persons had to go to Hunter for supplies, and he took all of us along. I was glad to go on this trip, for I wanted to buy a fishing line and some hooks. I had seen real trout in the stream by the rickety old bridge, and I had decided to catch them.

Early in the afternoon, when we got back from Hunter,

I cut a green birch pole and fixed it up with my new line and hooks. Then, after digging some worms and putting them in a tin can with some grass to keep them moist, I started out alone for the stream. In my pocket I carried a ruler, in order to measure the fish I caught and obey the law. It was unlawful to take a trout under six inches.

I had not been fishing very long when I had a bite, and up I pulled a small trout. But when I measured him he was too little; he was five and three quarters inches long! However, I just could not throw him back. I took him by head and tail and stretched him until he met the requirements of the law, and then I ran to the boardinghouse.

Mrs. Persons agreed that my fish was just within the law. And I stayed in the kitchen while she cleaned and floured him and got him ready for the frying pan. But since it was not yet dinner time she put him on a plate and set him in the milk house, where it was cool. Later when we went to get my trout, it was gone. The cat had got into the milk house, and all that we found were the head and tail.

Catching fish is always better than eating them; I didn't really mind, and the very next day I started out again. In fact, I liked fishing so much that day after day, with my tin can of worms and my green birch pole, I went to the stream by myself. I wandered up and down it until I located a deep pool beside a flat rock where I could sit. And hour after hour I fished. I caught many small fish, but I always hoped for a big one—a big one like those that I could see lying quietly at the bottom. Big fish, I reasoned, must get hungry like little ones. But somehow they never did. No matter how juicy the worm that I slowly dragged before them, the big fish never bit. They were all too old and wise. They would only turn and swim away.

But even though I never caught a big fish, I loved sitting on a flat rock by the stream all by myself. I loved the sound of the water as it rushed over the rocks, and the warm sun was soothing. Then all around me there were so many interesting things! On the surface of the water in quiet places I saw funny little insects skating. And I also noticed the beautiful color of the rocks, the mosses, the shimmer of the pebbles on the water's bottom, and the many little plants and grasses that grew along the shady edge.

It was peaceful here by the stream, and one could dream of all kinds of things—of inventions one would some day make, of wealth and power, of owning an automobile, of growing up and wearing long pants and, perhaps, some day speaking without a stammer.

Then, sitting here alone, one could also think of things close at hand. One could empty one's pockets and spread one's belongings out on the big flat rock. I divided my treasures into two piles. One pile I planned to keep. But the things in the other pile I planned to exchange with other boys. In this way I would get new treasures.

I would exchange my colored chalk and crayons, my pencil stubs, toothpicks, rubber bands, and paper clips, and even my piece of iridescent sea shell. But my other treasures I would keep. I would keep my pocket compass, the agate marble that was sherry-colored and streaked like a cat's eye, my horseshoe magnet, jackknife, chipped magnifying glass, and pocket mirror. These things I had to keep because they were essential to my life.

All of us had a wonderful time at Persons' Boarding House. There were so many things to do and so many things to eat! We had fresh milk and butter, eggs and cookies and homemade bread. Then every Sunday we had fricasseed chicken and ice cream. And all these things tasted extra good because we had a part in them.

We helped bring the cows in and watched them being milked, we saw Rip make the butter, and we gathered the eggs in the henhouse. And when the Sunday chickens had to be killed we were right there for the slaughter. We also helped make the ice cream; each took a turn at grinding the freezer.

Life on a farm, I thought, was just about as perfect as life could be. And for a brief moment I even thought that perhaps it was better than living on an enchanted island. But when I remembered that whole world of things I had left behind, I realized that I belonged in New York.

However, life here in the mountains was peaceful and pleasant. The days were sunny and filled with fun. The nights were still except for the katydids and crickets. And, up above, the sky was filled with silence and stars. Here one heard no noisy street sounds or cats fighting in the backyards.

Not all days were peaceful. Some were peppered with disasters, but they were soon over, and life again returned to its calm.

There was a day when Rip returned from the woods with his muzzle filled with porcupine quills, and Mr. Persons pulled them out one by one with a big pair of pliers. It was the only thing that Mr. Persons could do, and it was

very painful. With every pull poor Rip yelped and whined.
But he understood that Mr. Persons did not mean to harm
him, that he was helping him, and he did not try to run
away.

We children stood about and watched. We were in agony
at the whole painful sight, for we loved poor Rip. And we
were not so brave as he, for in a few minutes the quiet of
the countryside was broken as we burst out bawling at the
top of our lungs.

Mrs. Persons, hearing all this from the kitchen, came out
with a plate of cookies. We each took one and ate. Our
tears continued to flow, but with our mouths filled our bawling was muffled. At length the last quill was pulled, the
cookies were finished, Rip licked his chops, and all of us
smiled again.

Another day a cow was missing, and Rip was sent out to
find her. He was gone for some time, but at length we saw
him driving the unwilling cow home through the fields, nip-
ning her hind legs when she tarried.

And once the horses deserted our farm. They found
greener grass over the fence and did not want to come home
at all. We had to pull really hard on the halters to bring
them back. And we were mad because they were so disloyal.
But even when they were back in the barn they were still set
on mischief. One of them got loose from his stall and with
his nose he worked the tight cover off the feed barrel. He
ate almost half a barrel of grain before he was discovered!

I learned that on a farm one had to be constantly on the
lookout for such troubles. Mr. Persons told me that one winter a bear had come down from the woods and he had shot

him and shared the good bear meat with all his neighbors. Then there were other times when he had shot wildcats and foxes trying to raid his henhouse. And one day, after a rainstorm, I saw Mr. Persons kill a hawk that was hovering low over the chicken yard.

I saw him get his gun, and I followed. We hid in the woodshed, just inside the doorway, so that the hawk could not see us. Here we waited for almost half an hour as the hawk circled cautiously lower and lower. Finally he swooped down in a long curved flight, and the frightened chickens started running back and forth. It was then that Mr. Persons stepped out with his big gun and let go both barrels. The hawk fell dead to the ground.

I admired Mr. Persons for what he had done. There was something about it that I liked. Here was a man with a big gun in his hands defending his property from an unlawful raider. He was master of his farm.

Then suddenly, I don't know why, standing there looking at Mr. Persons, I thought of Grandpa and the cigar store. Grandpa could never have a gun and protect what was his. I wondered why. And then I found the answer.

Mr. Persons owned his farm—two hundred and forty acres, buildings, cattle, horses, machinery, wagons, trees. The very grass, the very earth belonged to him. The sun, the rain, the wind were there for him. And Grandpa, back home in New York, was in his store where the elevated structure blotted out the sun. He was there in his store, but it wasn't his. The building belonged to someone else. Almost everything he had belonged to someone else, even the beautiful telephone. Our telephone was not really ours: it belonged to the telephone company, and Grandpa paid rent for it each month.

Then, reasoning with myself, I thought that we too owned things: the furniture in the apartment upstairs, the old snuff jars, the happy Negro boy, the wooden Indian. But somehow, compared to Mr. Persons and his farm— For the first time in my life I had an empty feeling inside, and the ground under my feet fell away.

For the next four or five summers Grandma and I went to Persons' Boarding House. Each year I was older. And at the end of the last summer, when we returned to New York, I took over the job of going alone each night to Newspaper Row to deliver the classified advertisements.

That fall, too, I had my first suit with long pants, and I entered Stuyvesant High School.

4

Lady Liberty

OVER THE STAGE IN OUR ASSEMBLY
hall at Stuyvesant High School were carved the words,
"Know the Truth and It Shall Make You Free." In the
years that followed all America learned a lot of truth, and
if it helped to make us free, it also helped to make us very
uncomfortable. The truths we learned imposed changes.

These were to be years of great social change. These were
to be years when thousands upon thousands of immigrants
arrived from Europe; years when the great American fortunes were challenged, trusts were broken, labor organized,
the extremes of wealth and poverty reduced. In those years
the common man began to emerge. And out of these changes
a new society was born. Democracy was strengthened, and
America became a freer land.

In those days man's gateway to freedom was the Port of
New York.

Each week ships filled with immigrants arrived in our
harbor. These immigrants came from every country in Europe and the Near East. And it was a common sight, for
those of us who went downtown, to see them; men, women,
and children, cleareyed, with bright scrubbed faces, in pic-

turesque native costumes, carrying huge bundles and wicker
baskets. Each wore a large tag in his coat, and they all looked
about with wonder in their eyes.

One could always see such a crowd down at the immigration pier at the Battery, where they had just landed from
Ellis Island and passed through the immigration bureau.
Now they were standing huddled together on a street in
a new land—America.

I sometimes went down to watch them; I don't know why,
but I did. Some were met by friends and relatives, and they
cried. But others were alone—alone on a street of a strange
city in a new land. They looked frightened, and still there
was an eagerness about them.

There was always another group of people on the street
close to the immigration pier—people who had come on
business. There were housewives looking for servants, there
were agents from companies looking for labor, and there
were representatives of foreign-language communities all
over the country. There were men from the German communities in Milwaukee and St. Louis to guide and take care
of their countrymen. There were also representatives from
the Swedish colony in Minnesota, and from other foreign
colonies. Here, too, were company agents looking for strong
cheap labor for railroads, steel mills, coal mining companies,
and other heavy industry. They offered free transportation
and immediate work.

Some of the immigrants went off to join their countrymen
in different parts of America, some signed up as labor for
big industry, but many preferred to remain in New York
within the protection of their native districts. By this process

the foreign sections in the city swelled until they overlapped. But it made things gayer.

Each district became more distinctly a piece of the home country in Europe. Foreign-language newspapers were born. Our newsstands now carried papers in German, Yiddish, Czech, Italian, Greek—every major language of Europe. Foreign theaters also came into being. There were two German theaters, several Jewish theaters, one Italian theater; and the Chinese downtown had a little theater very beautifully decorated inside with golden dragons and carved lattice screens.

We who lived in New York often visited these foreign districts and ate the native food. For a five-cent ride on a trolley you could visit a slice of almost any country in the world. The restaurants were inexpensive and good. We learned to eat Italian spaghetti, Armenian shish kebab, Chinese-American chop suey, and goulash downtown where the Hungarians had entrenched themselves behind a whole rampart of Hungarian restaurants, gypsy music, paprika, and Tokay wine.

It was interesting to see the immigrants arrive in America and to visit their foreign districts. But I often wondered if I, in their place, should have had the courage to leave my homeland and the things I knew and come alone so far to a strange land to begin life again. I knew that what they left behind was often tyranny, poverty, and hopelessness. I knew that they came to opportunity and freedom. Yet it took strength and courage. And I wondered if I should have it. Then I thought of Grandpa. He had once been one of them.

"It all happened in Paris. I had escaped from the Czar."
Grandpa always began his story with these words. Then he
would continue: "I was strong, and I got a job in a factory.
I had to get a job, because I didn't have any money. I had
escaped across the border at night."

At this point of the story I always asked: "Were you
alone, Grandpa?"

"No, I was not alone. There were five of us. And each of
us had to pay the guide who smuggled us through the woods
at night across the border. Each one of us paid him what in
America would be twenty-five dollars. It was a lot of money,
and I had worked hard to save it. It was all the money I had,
and so when I was safe across the Russian border I was
penniless. But I was happy, because I was free. I was determined to get to America. The first step had been accomplished."

Then Grandpa would tell how he had worked at odd jobs
for his food and lodging, all the time making his way slowly
across Europe until he reached Paris.

"In Paris," he said, "I went to work in a brass foundry.
It was a good job, not too hard, and I earned a fair wage,
enough so that I could live and at the same time put aside a
little each week for my boat fare to America. The only trouble with the job was that it was very monotonous. All day
long I had to file the casting seams off brass faucets. It was
just one faucet after another. You never saw so many. Day
after day, faucets and more faucets."

At this point in his story Grandpa always paused. Then
he would continue:

"Yes, it was a tedious job, and I did not know how much

longer I could stand it, when one day everything changed. One day when I came to work, the foreman took me down the hall and into a large room, and there on a wooden platform stood a great bronze casting. It rose up almost to the ceiling of the room in a huge shapeless mass. But I didn't ask any questions. I knew what I was supposed to do: file off the casting seams. I set to work. I got a ladder, and I started from the top and worked down."

Here there was another pause in the story.

"No, I never knew what I was working on until a long time later. I did ask the foreman two or three times, but he wouldn't tell me. He said that this was a special job and he was not allowed to talk about it. So I worked on day after day, filing off the seams and cleaning off the encrusted sand. I was glad to be working at something else besides faucets.

"And then, one day when I had finally reached the bottom of the casting and I was knocking and brushing off hardened sand, I discovered a whole set of toes! I stood back and looked at the casting. It was a foot!—the biggest foot I had ever seen. I wondered and wondered what use it could ever be. But since I couldn't figure it out, I went back to work. Now that I knew I was working on a foot I was more interested. I cleaned each toe and I filed every toenail. I did a real good job. Even the foreman said it was good. And all the time I worked I kept asking myself 'What good is such a foot, what use is it?' But I wasn't able to figure it out."

At this point Grandpa would pause to gather his strength for the last and best part of his story.

"Well, right after I finished working on this foot," he would continue, "I left Paris and went to London. I worked there for almost two years, and at last I had money enough to come to America. I got on the steamer at Southampton, and we started out across the Atlantic. It was a long voyage and a rough one, but I didn't care, because now I was only a few days away from America.

"Then one day, at last, we steamed into New York Harbor and past the Statute of Liberty; and there, big as life, was my foot!"

With this Grandpa's story ended. He always smiled proudly and then he would add: "All this happened while I was seeking liberty. There I was filing away on the toenails of Lady Liberty herself, and I didn't even know it."

Immigration, the Statue of Liberty, religious and political freedom were one thing, but full freedom was another. With the sudden growth of industry in America man had to fight for a new freedom: economic freedom.

During the early years of the new century we witnessed the first mass stirring of labor in America. During these years we began to learn the first truths about the relationship of men, machines, and wealth. What we learned were usually bitter truths, and these truths disturbed the calm surface of the life we had known. They made us uncomfortable.

Hardly a week passed in which our papers and periodicals did not record troublesome events—an attempted strike in Pittsburgh, protest against child labor in the cotton mills, a report on tuberculosis among coal miners and their families. Such articles appeared with persistent regularity, and the very air we breathed was troubled. The words "labor," "capital," "industrial revolution," "strike" and "living wage" were heard everywhere, even in Grandpa's cigar store.

Of course it was Mr. Hadley who had the most to say about these issues, and the things he said made Grandpa so angry that I have never forgotten them. And, thanks to the rub between the two, my interest in these matters was first awakened.

Now, Grandpa and Mr. Hadley really agreed on most questions: they differed only on the method of reform. Grandpa agreed that it was very wrong for little children of eight and nine to work twelve hours at machines in the cotton mills. In fact, he thought that there should be no child labor at all in America. He also agreed that there should be laws to protect women in industry and that all labor, if worth its hire, was worth a living wage. On such points Grandpa and Mr. Hadley agreed, but they disagreed on the remedy. Grandpa felt that the industrialists would in time understand the problems and institute the necessary reforms. But Mr. Hadley quarreled with this reasoning.

"The only hope for the workingman in America," he said, "is for labor to organize into unions. The industrialists will never understand, nor will they be moved by reason. They are blinded by greed. They must be made to feel the force of collective action. Unless labor organizes, it will be ground underfoot. And even when labor does organize it will have to fight every inch of the way. It will take years and years."

Then, in an attempt to get Grandpa to understand what was going on, Mr. Hadley would speak about the industrial revolution and how the machine had displaced the workingman. He explained very carefully the problems that resulted from this displacement. And he said that these problems would continue for a long time, because in the future the machine was bound to become more and more important in industry. He said that the industrialists, although they were greedy, were not really to blame; they were only taking advantage of a situation. But, human nature being what it was, the Morgans, the Rockefellers, the Carnegies, and the Fricks were not going to surrender anything willingly. Labor would have to fight for the right to survive.

Grandpa did not like the word "fight." He was for peace at any cost. But I felt differently about fighting; besides, lots of things that I heard Mr. Hadley say sounded all right to me. Now that I was older and in high school and reminded every morning that somewhere hidden there is a truth that would make me free, I began to search. I began to read a great deal.

When I was younger I liked books with pictures like those in Dante's Inferno illustrated by Doré. I never read the text, but I spent long hours looking at the pictures of the tortures of hell. They were wonderful. Now, I read the words in books. The illustrations, if there were any, did not mean so much to me. But there was no order or system to my reading; it was just hit and miss. I read everything I could lay my hands on, newspapers, periodicals, and books.

I read how the Count of Monte Cristo finally escaped from his dungeon, and I learned that house servants in New York earned sixteen dollars a month. I traveled through Old Spain with Don Quixote and Sancho, charging windmills and defending fair ladies. I solved mysteries with Sherlock Holmes, and I learned how Jay Gould and Jim Fisk, two American millionaires, manipulated the gold market for their own benefit and caused the financial panic of Black Friday. I read how workers in America were now asking that the working day be cut from ten, twelve, and more hours a day to eight hours. I also read that some groups were asking for compensation for injuries sustained on the job. I read *Treasure Island, Dr. Jekyll and Mr. Hyde,* and *The Call of the Wild.* And I also read of "extremists" who were speaking of unemployment compensation and old age pensions, of "agitators" who were organizing labor, of "crackpots" and "hopeless idealists." I read *David Harum,* and I also read how J. P. Morgan made a great profit selling rifles that he knew were defective to the U.S. Government during the Civil War.

I mixed my fiction with facts. I read a little of everything. And there was a great deal for me to read, because, besides the hundreds of famous classics, new books were constantly appearing that were related to the unsettled spirit of our time. In 1901 there appeared a *History of Tammany Hall,* by Gustavus Myers, disclosing the deep corruption of our New York City politics. In the same year a young writer in San Francisco, Frank Norris, published *The Octopus.* This book showed how the great railroads of America were strangling the farmer, and it led to a federal investigation of railroad combines. In 1903 Norris published a second book called *The Pit,* which exposed the dishonest manipulations of the Chicago grain market. This also led to a federal investigation of grain manipulation. These investigations were sensational. The public was horrified at what was disclosed.

In 1904 a woman by the name of Ida Tarbell published *A History of the Standard Oil Company.* In this book she revealed to the public the corruption of this monopoly. In this same year a New York journalist, Lincoln Steffens, exposed municipal corruption throughout the country in his *Shame of the Cities.* In 1906 the whole country was shaken by another sensational book, *The Jungle.* As Norris had exposed the corruption of railroads and wheat market, Upton Sinclair now exposed the corruption of the Chicago meat-packing industry. Again there was a federal investigation that made the headlines of all the newspapers across the country.

Many of these books I did not read, but I knew about them, because I read the papers; besides, everyone who came into Grandpa's cigar store discussed them. Not only did Mr. Hadley discuss these books, but also the firemen and policemen and many of our other customers. It was surprising how interested everyone was. There were all kinds of opinions and endless discussions. And for the first time in my life I began to understand the force of the printed word.

In the years that followed there were more books. In 1907 Jack London, who had risen to fame and popularity with stories of the Klondike days, now wrote *The Iron Heel.* In this book he presented a picture of America twenty-five years in the future. He showed it as a land ruled by monopolies that had succeeded in stamping out all our democratic institutions and all the freedoms guaranteed by our Constitution. This book made a deep impression on a vast American public, for in it they saw the truth. It was frightening.

Then in 1910 there appeared *A History of the Great*

American Fortunes. This book by Gustavus Myers tore away the veil of respectability from such names as Sage, Vanderbilt, Blair, Frick, Carnegie, Hill, and many others. It told page by page, fact by fact, how these great fortunes had been made through manipulation, corruption, fraud, and lawlessness.

Of course, there were other books published during these years, but these were the books that were related to the spirit of the time. These were the books people spoke about. Through these books the American public learned the truth about a very ugly section of America. We no longer heard the names of millionaires with awe and respect. We looked with suspicion at such gifts as public libraries by men like Carnegie, who had amassed their millions by doubtful methods. We wanted America freed; we wanted America to belong to the people of America, not to a handful of corrupt men. Public opinion, during these "muckraking" years, had turned against the strangle hold of big industry. The public was seeking reforms, an ethical code to cover the relationship of industry and the people.

And it was at this time that big business in America lost the respect of the public. The public trust that was lost, it never regained. And it was at this time also that big business found it necessary to engage a friendly go-between known as a Public Relations Counselor, to try to win back the confidence of the people.

At this time, too, the workingman became more articulate. Unions were organized and began to grow in strength. Man was trying to find his place in the machine age. He was seeking a fair relationship between himself and industry. Those who held economic power were very reluctant to give it up, and so there were many violent struggles.

All these developments disturbed Grandpa's peace. He felt that such agitation was undermining society. But Mr. Hadley said that it was all to the good. He said that industry and machinery were in themselves good, but that they must not be allowed to grind man to a pulp. If man allowed machinery to crush him, then what good was freedom of speech, freedom of religion, freedom of the press? Grandpa didn't agree with this kind of talk at all, and he wished that Mr. Hadley would take his tobacco trade somewhere else.

But I agreed with Mr. Hadley, because of many things I had read, and because, right on our block, I came to know two men who had lost their freedom. And it all came about through Grandpa's bunions.

Grandpa was badly troubled with corns and bunions. On certain days his feet hurt him so that he padded around the cigar store in carpet slippers. One evening he said casually: "I think I am going to let Mr. Schiller down the street build me a proper pair of shoes."

My grandmother did not answer him directly; she spoke to me instead. "Your grandfather must think he's a rich man," she said. "It costs at least seven dollars to have a pair of shoes made to order, and you can buy a ready-made pair for two-fifty." With this remark Grandpa's suggestion was vetoed. And the result was that on rainy days my grandfather complained bitterly about his feet. They did really hurt him. And so in the end Grandma softened and rescinded her veto.

I went with my grandfather to order the shoes, and that's how I first met Mr. Schiller. He was an old man with gray hair and big knotted hands. He spoke with a German accent.

His shop was one flight down in a basement near the corner of Fifty-first Street. It was a dark little shop with only one window, and the light filtered through a street grill above. People passing along Third Avenue would never have known that there was a shoemaker's shop down there in the cellar were it not for a golden boot that hung over the steps.

Mr. Schiller examined every corn and bunion on Grandpa's feet, and, after studying the problem very carefully, he had Grandpa stand with one foot on each page of an open ledger. He took tracings of both feet. Then with a tape measure he measured the different parts of each foot, and with a wooden T-square he calculated the various heights along the insteps. These he recorded in the ledger. After this he made sketches of each bunion.

Grandpa was now ready to go, but I asked Mr. Schiller if I might stay and watch. He took a pair of wooden lasts and started to make them into exact copies of Grandpa's feet. With a sharp knife he scraped away in places and he built up other parts with bits of leather. Then he made a model of each bunion and tacked it in its proper place. He was painstaking, and it took a long time before he had the forms finished. He worked all afternoon on this, and the next day Grandpa had to come so that the models could be checked. They needed very little adjusting.

In the days that followed I spent many hours in Mr. Schiller's shop watching him work.

"They don't make many shoes to order any more, do they, Mr. Schiller?"

"No, they don't," he replied. "Everything is machine-made. Boston."

"It's a big business, manufacturing shoes."

"It grew big. In the old days all shoes were made by hand. Now they punch them out quickly. I hear that in some of the big Boston factories they produce one pair of shoes every minute."

"With so many shoes being made one would think that everyone in New York would have at least one pair."

"Yes. One would think so," he replied.

"But lots of people don't have shoes. Early in the morning when the laborers go to work I see many of them with burlap bags tied around their feet."

"It's not only in New York," he said. "It's everywhere; everywhere in the world."

In time Grandpa's shoes were finished. It had taken Mr. Schiller the greater part of a week to make them, and they cost seven dollars. But they were good shoes. Grandpa smiled and said he was walking on clouds. They wore like iron. And they lasted Grandpa for years and years. Even after they had been mended two or three times they were still good.

After Grandpa's shoes were finished I still visited Mr. Schiller. I sat beside his bench and watched him work. It was interesting to see him cut leather with a knife and fit and shape the pieces to the lasts. And it was interesting to watch him stitch a sole. He used several lengths of heavy cotton thread, which he waxed very thoroughly. To each end of this thread he attached a bristle, as long and as sharp as a cat's whisker and as stiff as wire. These enabled him to pass the thread back and forth through the holes he made with his awl. The ends of the thread were so twisted around the bristles that they seemed almost welded together.

I liked to visit Mr. Schiller and watch everything he did. I liked his shop with its smell of leather and glue and the shelves filled with wooden lasts, each tagged with a customer's name. I liked the nails, the hammers, the big ledgers with foot tracings. I liked Mr. Schiller. Hours on end I sat and watched as he plied his craft.

"I am not a cobbler," he often said. "I am a shoemaker."

He had been trained in Europe, and he took great pride in his work. But with the change in times his business had fallen off, and most of his work was now repairing soles and heels. He felt this change as indignity and degradation. Yet he was glad of any little job.

However, occasionally someone with a deformed foot would climb down the cellar stairs and order a pair of shoes. When this happened Mr. Schiller was happy. This was not cobbler's work, this was the kind of work he liked doing.

As he worked he talked. He told me many stories of his boyhood in Germany. It was a happy life, and as he recalled it we laughed together. But one day he spoke of something else: he spoke of his military service in the Kaiser's army.

"I was not alone," he said. "It was the same for everyone. You in America would not know about it, but in Germany, and in all the other countries in Europe, when a young fellow gets to a certain age then he must go in the army."

"For long?"

"Three years."

"And you didn't like it?"

"No," he cried, and he banged down so hard with his hammer that he broke the handle.

Little by little I learned that the time he spent in the German Army had warped his entire life. And he spoke of military caste and of his officers with great hatred. Often he repeated: "Common soldiers are treated worse than swine!"

"And when you finished serving your time, what did you do?"

"I was free. I took every penny I had and went straight to Hamburg and bought a steerage ticket for America. I did not even go home to say good-bye. I wrote them a letter. Let them have their Kaiser!"

He spoke with anger, even about the Kaiser. And I didn't understand. "The Kaiser is a good man," I said.

"Good man! That's what you read in the newspapers. The Kaiser is a pig."

I was shocked. This was the first time I had heard anyone speak so disrespectfully of a ruler. And I did not know if a shoemaker, even though he were skilled in his trade, had the right to hurl abuse at someone who wore a crown.

"You wouldn't understand: you are an American boy. But in my country no one is free, no one can speak as he likes. Everyone is registered and numbered. The police and the military at all times know where you are. And as your father was, so you must be. If you were born a peasant, you remain a peasant. It is almost impossible to better your condition, but whatever your condition, you belong to the Kaiser. You are not free."

Now his anger seemed to leave him, and he spoke of America and how, even though he had had to work hard, he had lived as he liked. No one had bothered him. He went where he liked, he spoke as he liked. And in time he owned a nice shop and he had many good customers. He made fine custom shoes, the best in New York.

One day he spoke like this, but on other days he spoke of other things. He spoke about men and the values of life, he spoke about living from day to day, and he spoke about the relations of man to man. He spoke simply of things that were not simple. He was an uneducated person, but he seemed to know a great deal.

There was only one thing that he could not understand, and I did not know the answer. He could not understand why he, a man with training, skill, and the willingness to work, had been squeezed out by the factories in Boston. He could not understand why he had been reduced to this cellar room with only one window looking up through a grating to the sidewalk above.

"I feel like a prisoner, condemned. And yet I am a free man."

I had been visiting Mr. Schiller for many weeks before I knew that there was another craftsman down there in the cellar. His shop was in the back, with a window facing the yard. He was an Englishman named Mr. Corbet, and I soon came to know him, too.

Corbet and Schiller had a great deal in common, and still they were very different. Both had come to America as young men, both were skilled craftsmen who had once been wanted and were now cast aside. Schiller had been replaced by the machine; Corbet had been discarded because of age. He had worked for many years in the Steinway piano factory on Park Avenue, and when he was fifty he was considered too old. A younger man was hired to take his place.

Unlike Schiller, Mr. Corbet seldom spoke, and when he did speak he seemed devoid of imagination and philosophy. But he was a kind man and friendly. He taught me a great deal about different woods and how they were used. He taught me to distinguish freshly cut woods by the smell, and he explained to me the meaning of quartered oak and how first cutting the log in quarters brings out the free-flowing grain. He explained each tool and its use. And he let me watch him hour after hour as he planed his wood, ripped his boards, and dovetailed his joints. The whine of his plane and the taps of his hammer were happy sounds, but they were not often heard, for he had little work.

I learned a great deal about carpentry and cabinetmaking by watching Mr. Corbet. And I also learned that he, like Mr. Schiller, was a victim of our changing times. These were only two men, but I knew that there were many more who had come to America and found what they were seeking, hope and opportunity, only to see it taken away from them.

The thought that there were those whose lives were extinguished before they were over, those who carried their corpses with them before they found a grave, plagued me.

But while Schiller and Corbet and thousands of others were going down, their passing was not unnoticed. In Washington Theodore Roosevelt was President. He was a man of intelligence and vision, and he understood the new problems that faced America. And he was doing something about them.

Roosevelt became President by accident. After returning, a great hero, from the Spanish-American War, he was elected Governor of New York State in 1898. But he served only one term, for the political bosses found him honest and obstinate. He refused to take orders, and he was determined to serve the state for the best interests of the people. Therefore the bosses wanted to bury him politically, and they had him nominated as Vice-President on the Republican ticket with McKinley. As Vice-President he would become almost powerless and unable to block such legislation as the leaders desired to put through.

In this way, at the very start of the century, 1900, Theodore Roosevelt became Vice-President. Six months later President McKinley was assassinated at the World's Fair in Buffalo, and Roosevelt became President of the United States. He was forty-two years old.

He was a man of great personal charm and vitality. He was filled with enthusiasm, and he loved a good fight. And from the very first he fought for the rights of the everyday American; he became the "champion of the little man." And from the very first the people of America rallied to him. He was their man, and they knew it.

Theodore Roosevelt recognized completely the growing need for social reform in America. He was violent in his denunciations of the abuses of big business, industrialists, and other "malefactors of great wealth."

In his first message to Congress he championed the rights of labor to better its condition and gave sharp warning to illegal combinations of great corporations that were against the public interest. This was the opening blow of his "trust-busting." From that moment on his spirit of reform never slackened. He did not want to destroy big business in America: he simply wanted it regulated for the benefit of the whole country, for he understood clearly that if this were not done, industry would in time destroy itself and America too.

The great wave of "muckraking" literature and other exposés gave impetus to his political reforms. He instituted suits and investigations against the U.S. Steel Corporation, the Standard Oil Company, coal-mining and railroad and sugar interests, meat packers, and other abusive forces. One company alone, Standard Oil, was fined $29,000,000.

The fat that he hurled into the fire burned with a bright flame. And there were many in this land who were made uncomfortable. They did not want to surrender one straw of their ill-gotten power. They fought President Roosevelt at every step; they vilified him. But to the American public he was Teddy Roosevelt. And in 1904 he was elected President by an overwhelming majority.

During Roosevelt's two terms an ethical force swept over the country, and it had full public support. Enterprise had made itself too free, and the government was forced to step in to protect the people. The Sherman Antitrust Act was put into effect. The Pure Food and Drugs Act was passed. Companies were no longer allowed to sell adulterated food in cans under false labels. The meat packers and drug manufacturers were also, by this act, put under strict regulation. Bad meat and fake medicines were driven off the market. And overnight it became wrong to print misleading advertising or use the mails to defraud.

These were exciting years, and I was old enough to understand a good bit of what was going on. At any rate I learned a lot of truths.

But the full meaning and significance of what was happening did not come to us until much later. While these events were making history, we who were living through this time hardly realized the importance of what was happening. To have understood completely the meaning of the changes through which we were living would have taken a good deal of vision. And most of us were unaware of the great advances that were made.

Only later did we understand how important this time was. For it was during these years that the common man in America took a great stride forward. The government came to his defense, passed laws for his protection, and strengthened his rights. He became a freer man. And the new freedoms that he gained at this time he has never surrendered. Democracy was strengthened.

5

A Bushel of Experience

DURING MY FOUR YEARS IN HIGH school Theodore Roosevelt was in the White House. And he kept things boiling at a lively pace. I was interested in these world-shaking events, but I was interested in other things also—private things that concerned only me. I was my own "little man."

And while I was studying all kinds of stuffy things in school like algebra, German, and geometry, I was busy with important outside activities like racing, acting, theatergoing, and music. I was so good at some of these that I actually won three medals. Two of these, it is true, were of bronze; but one was made of solid silver.

I won the bronze medals for running and jumping. I won the silver medal during my last year in High School from the *New York Times*.

My interest in running dated back to my earliest years. In fact, by the time the Spanish-American War broke out I had already been running for a number of years. And during the war I spent a good deal of time practicing to become a runner for the U.S. Army; I had dreamed of delivering the second Message to Garcia. And had that sergeant with the red mustache at the recruiting station not deserted Reinhardt and me, I am sure I should have distinguished myself and received a medal back in those early days.

Through the years that followed I occasionally practiced running with other boys in Central Park. But we were all amateurs, and no reward ever awaited us at the finish line. There were no contests, no medals. Through the years I trained, but to what end? I became discouraged. I began to think that I should never have my chance. But life has a way of withholding its rewards. And on the very first day that I entered Stuyvesant High School I found the answer to my dream.

Stuyvesant High School was a brand-new school in a brand-new building. It was the first manual training high school to be opened in the city. It prepared boys for engineering and science and specialized in chemistry, physics, and various crafts. My class was the second to be enrolled, and when we arrived on the first day the building was still unfinished. There were packing cases in the halls and workmen everywhere.

On this day I joined a small group of boys and we wandered through the building, room after room. It was a wonderful place. Besides the regular classrooms there were physics and chemistry laboratories, a carpenter shop, a machine shop, and a room with at least thirty forges for metal work. But the very best place of all was a running track, the only indoor running track I had ever seen. It was cushioned and covered with a skidproof canvas, and the curves were sharply banked. As I looked at it my feet started itching. I could easily see that on such a track one could run like a streak. And right then and there I decided that this was the subject in which I would specialize.

The very next day I brought my running pants and sneakers to school and went to see the athletic instructor, Mr. Holton. He was a very nice man, and he understood my position right away. We discussed the situation, and he decided that I might be a good boy for the 110-pound relay team. That is how it all began.

Before I was able to do the first problem in algebra or the first lesson in German, before I had finished the first chapter of *Ivanhoe*, I was on the track team. It was obvious that my best talents were not in my head, but in my feet.

Being a member of the track team was not an easy thing to achieve. Only the best runners were chosen. And one had to win in competition against many boys. But I was determined. Now for the first time in my life my running had a goal; as a member of the team I should wear the school letters S.H.S. in red, sewn on my blue running shirt, and I should also be running in contests with other high schools for the honor of Stuyvesant.

During the winter we practiced on our indoor track, but in the spring and fall we went to a nearby park and ran on a cinder track.

Mr. Holton was a very good coach and he trained us carefully. We listened to every word he had to say and tried hard to follow his instructions. He showed us good form and style, and all of us improved a great deal. In time some of our boys won top honors in the interscholastic meets. The very first year my relay team won third place in a competition in one of the big armories. That is how I got my first bronze medal.

I was very proud and so encouraged that I decided to try my feet at broad jumping. I practiced a little, and at our next handicap meet I entered the contest. I guess Mr. Holton, when he looked me over, made a mistake and gave me too much handicap. He gave me four feet, and this, added to my 11-foot jump, brought me into third place.

That day I was decorated for the second time with a bronze medal. I was very happy, and I didn't care at all how things were going with Ivanhoe and Rowena.

Next to running, the theater was my greatest passion. And whenever I had twenty-five cents saved up I hurried over to Broadway. To be on time I had to leave school an hour early, but what learning could one miss in an hour?

Once on Broadway, with ninety theaters to choose from, I could always count on a lively afternoon. My mood dictated my choice. I could see serious drama, melodrama, comedy, a musical, burlesque, or vaudeville. I preferred drama and vaudeville.

I saw plays by Shakespeare, Sheridan, Ibsen, Oscar Wilde, and Pinero. I saw performances of *Uncle Tom's Cabin, The Count of Monte Cristo,* such melodramas as *Nelly the Beautiful Cloak Model,* and polite comedies such as *My American Cousin,* the play Lincoln was witnessing on the night when he was assassinated. In every one of these plays there were scenes that were unforgettable, such as Eliza crossing the ice and James K. Hackett fighting his way, sword in hand, down a stairway in *A Gentleman of France.* Before the curtain fell twenty dead bodies were strewn on the stage, Hackett was unscratched, and the audience was going wild.

I loved the theater. It was so packed with real life, conflict, honor, and oratory! And, besides, I mingled with so many interesting people! Of course, in reality I was in the first row from the ceiling, sitting high with the painted angels, and the interesting people were far below on the stage. But as soon as the curtain went up the distance between us melted, and there I was with Sir Johnston Forbes-Robertson in Elsinore in ancient Denmark. I went to Norway, France, England; I visited castles, had tea in drawing rooms, fought on battlefields, looked into strange bedrooms, and suffered in dark dungeons. I went to all these places with Sarah Bernhardt, John Drew, Mrs. Patrick Campbell, E. H. Sothern, Mrs. Fiske, Maude Adams, Robert Mantell, Otis Skinner, the young Ethel Barrymore, and her brothers Lionel and John.

Through vaudeville I came to know Lillian Russell, Weber and Fields, Montgomery and Stone, Will Rogers, Sophie Tucker, McIntyre and Heath, Rock and Fulton, George M. Cohan, Houdini, W. C. Fields, and a host of others.

All these people were my friends. Though they didn't know me, I knew them. And as a friend I cheered and clapped.

It was in vaudeville that I first saw great acts of magic, famous acrobats, trick bicycle riders, and dancers. It was there that I first heard the English comedienne, Vesta Victoria, sing "There was I, waiting at the Church" and Harry Lauder in kilts sing his famous Scottish songs. There Will Rogers did his roping act, W. C. Fields gave his mad per-

formance at the billiard table, and George M. Cohan, with
his father, mother, and sister, sang and danced. It was in
vaudeville that I heard De Wolf Hopper recite "Casey At
the Bat" and the dynamic and riotous Maggie Cline, "Queen
of Ireland," do "Throw 'Em Down, McCluskey."

Vaudeville was very popular. The four or five vaudeville
theaters in the city were constantly packed with enthusiastic
audiences. But these audiences were also very critical. They
knew what was good, they wanted the best, and they wanted
it quickly. They booed and hissed anyone who did not meet
their standards, and their favorites were never allowed to
leave the stage before they had given those popular numbers
for which they were known. Vaudeville entertainment was
compressed: one act followed another without a moment's
delay. And each artist had to capture the audience in the very
moment he stepped upon the stage. The acts were short, usually from ten to twenty minutes. There was no time for dally-
ing. Every performance was an onslaught, a direct attack,
quickly on and quickly over.

There were not many actors who could meet such exacting
demands. It took training, timing, and talent. Some of the
greatest performers of all time belonged to vaudeville. And
two of the greatest were Bert Williams and Charlie Chaplin.

Bert Williams was a supreme artist and unforgettable. He
was a Negro, and he appeared on stage in blackface with
large white mouth and sad eyes. He dressed in an ill-fitting
black suit with loose white gloves. He was long and lean and
walked with a disjointed shuffle. His voice was low and
melodious. He personified the pathetic in life. He was the
forgotten man. And the more forgotten he was, the funnier

he was. From the moment he stepped out from the wings the house was still and the air electrified. He would shuffle across the stage until he came close to the footlights; then, leaning over, with big full sad eyes, he would confide in the audience.

> *Two ivory cubes*
> *With ebony dots*
> *Oft lead to pistol shots*
> *And cemetery lots.*

And with such a simple beginning his act was on.

Bert Williams had many songs and routines. One of his best was a poker game in pantomine. In this act he played an imaginary game of poker with imaginary companions and imaginary cards. He sat alone in the center of the stage, slowly dealing out the cards one at a time and studying each player. Five times he dealt around; then stealthily he picked up his cards and studied his hand, all the time casting suspicious glances at his companions. Now he laid down his hand and dealt the extra cards. He was always pleased to give out three cards, curious when a player drew two, and filled with misgivings when someone drew one. In the end he drew two for himself, and one could see that they were just the cards he needed. Now some lively betting started; and soon, so confident was he, his whole stack of chips was in the pot. Then came the moment for call, and he would get ready to rake in the winnings. But suddenly there was a turn of events. He craned his neck and looked and looked. He had lost! And his face and body became those of the saddest man in the whole world. We felt his bitter disappointment, but we roared with laughter—laughter mingled with tears.

His act was never finished unless he sang his famous song, "Nobody." It was a long song, and this is one of the stanzas:

> *And in that recent railroad wreck,*
> *Who took that en–gine off my neck?*
> *Who? Nobody.*
> *And I done nothin' to nobody,*
> *And nobody never done nothin' for me.*

Bert Williams was ever the injured one, the loser, the one for whom life is utterly unfair. But he always managed to shuffle on through life, touching, and lovable. There were many who gave imitations of Bert Williams, and they did achieve his walk, his loose-jointed shuffle, his low, soft voice. But there was always a little something missing: his genius.

Charlie Chaplin first came to America with a small English music-hall company eight or nine years after the turn of the century. He did two acts, "A Night's Lodging" and "The Music Hall." Both in pantomine, they were so popular that they played for a long time.

The scene of "A Night's Lodging" was an English flophouse. The stage was set with two rows of wooden cots of the crudest kind. When the curtain goes up it is evening, and the vagrants begin arriving. Many beds are soon filled. An old beggar now enters and finds his cot. Then suddenly Charlie appears, a cockney sharper with a quick step and glance and bad intentions. In one moment he has surveyed the place, and he picks the bed next to the old beggar.

All is now dark and the men are snoring; all except the old beggar and Charlie. The old beggar is restless, and Charlie, peering from under his blanket, watches him carefully. The beggar, certain that everyone is asleep, now, takes out his bag of coins and, spreading them carefully on the blanket, begins counting them. Charlie, seeing this performance, quickly devises a plan. He quietly rolls under his own bed, draws a coin from his pocket (the only one he has), and rings it soundly on the floor. The old miser, thinking that one of his coins has dropped, gets out of bed and on his hands and knees starts groping along the floor in the dark. At this Charlie makes a bold raid on the beggar's coins, takes purse and all, and gets back into his bed.

As soon as the beggar discovers his loss he becomes frenzied and goes from bed to bed waking up the men, pulling off the blankets, searching everywhere. There are a lot of arguments and there is a lot of confusion. And many of the men get out of bed to fight with the old beggar. In the meantime Charlie, the foxy cockney, taking advantage of this confusion, eludes the old miser by sneaking in and out of one bed after another. He finally works his way to the door and escapes with the bag of coins.

In "The Music Hall" Charlie Chaplin played the part of a drunken dude. The dude, with a red nose and a white carnation, staggers into the stage box of a music hall. In his drunken stupor he applauds at the wrong time and interrupts everything and everybody. He makes himself generally obnoxious. During one act he becomes so enthusiastic that he tries to climb out of the box and on to the stage. He is restrained with difficulty. Now and then he falls asleep, and

the show goes on peacefully. But suddenly he awakens again
with a start and carries on where he left off.

These were the two pantomime acts that introduced
Charlie Chaplin to American audiences. They appeared just
before the big shoes, loose pants, bamboo cane, and derby
hat that labeled Charlie's little man and brought him world
fame. But, even without the big shoes and the derby hat,
those of us in New York who saw this English comedian
felt at once the strength and power of his artistry.

There were other great artists besides Bert Williams and
Charlie Chaplin, but these two were supreme.

The theater was exciting. It was an important part of our
lives, and it was our only real source of entertainment. The
motion pictures were fun, but they were mostly slapstick.
In the theater one saw great drama and great artists. The
theater was a living art in which the public took a definite
interest. Often after a performance those who came out
would stand around on the sidewalks and have heated discussions about the play they had just seen and the merits
of this or that actor or actress.

Thus, the hour that I lost in school was used to great advantage. I learned things in the theater that I should have
learned nowhere else. It was here that I was introduced to
some of the world's greatest literature. And it was brought
to life for me by many of the most famous actors and
actresses of all time. Through their interpretations I was
given the emotional essence of life. I also learned from
vaudeville; for the comic, too, has its human values. These
things I could certainly not have learned in school. And,
besides, while learning I enjoyed every minute.

I liked the theater. I liked actors. And now and again, just to discuss the state of the current drama and gather up the loose ends of professional opinion, I visited Mr. Quaff at the actors' boardinghouse on Lexington Avenue near Fiftieth Street.

One day, right in the middle of a very interesting conversation on Ibsen, Mr. Quaff suddenly asked: "Why don't you study acting? You'd like to get rid of your stammer, wouldn't you?"

I quickly nodded my head. Of course I wanted to get rid of my stammer. And if I could be an actor too—!

"An actor has to talk and talk properly," continued Mr. Quaff. "Learn to be an actor. Stammering is only a habit, a bad habit."

I agreed with him, but said nothing.

"Do you know where they teach acting free of charge?"

No. I did not know.

"Well, I'll tell you. You go downtown to this place." He wrote the name and address on his card. "You ask for Emma Sheridan and give her my card. We were once stranded with a company in Montana. She'll remember me all right. Emma Sheridan directs plays down there. It's an organization run by society ladies."

I had the card in my pocket for several days and almost wore off the pencil markings before I decided to use it. I was curious about this place, and yet I hesitated, for my speech was so unreliable. I had good days when I could recite fairly well in the backyard by myself, but faced with an audience of one or more—

One day, however, after school, I drew the card out and,

blowing up my courage, ran downtown and found the place. But suddenly my confidence was gone and I did not dare go in. I stood on the sidewalk outside. I didn't dare go in, and still I didn't want to go away.

As I stood there I saw a lot of other boys and girls going into the building. Some looked very nice and others looked like simpletons. And, seeing the simpletons, I figured that I was as good as they were. After all, I only stammered; I wasn't cockeyed, bowlegged, or feeble-minded. I took courage and went through the front door.

As I came into the entrance hall a young girl pointed at me and said: "Look! Here's a new boy." Then, coming up to me she said: "Go into that room and speak to Mrs. Hirsh. She takes care of all the new kids."

Mrs. Hirsh was a nice woman with a big bosom on which was pinned a small gold watch. I was sure she must be one of the society ladies that Mr. Quaff had spoken about. We had a long talk together, and she asked me a lot of questions about myself and my family. She was interested in my grandfather's cigar store and his agency for classified advertisements. And I told her how each evening I went down to the newspaper offices on Park Row. Then she asked me what I wanted to do in the theater. I was surprised. I said that I wanted to be an actor, of course.

She looked very serious, and then she said: "We have so many actors! Everyone wants to be an actor. But you know the theater is a lot more than that. The curtain can't be raised without carpenters, painters, designers, scene shifters, property men, and electricians. These are all very important jobs."

She looked at me and waited.

I shook my head. No. I wanted to be an actor.

She smiled, and then she said: "When Miss Sheridan comes she will speak with you."

Miss Sheridan soon arrived. She was a little person in her early forties, very pretty and attractively dressed. Her voice was deep and expressive.

I overheard Mrs. Hirsh say to her: "We have a new boy; he just came in."

"Good, we need boys."

"You'll have to talk with him first."

"Why? What's wrong with him?"

"Well— Just talk with him. He comes from a broken home."

Mrs. Hirsh and Miss Sheridan didn't say any more. And this was the first time I had heard the expression "broken home." I wondered what she meant by calling my home "broken." Then I remembered that when Mrs. Hirsh had asked me about my parents I had told her they were divorced.

Miss Sheridan came over to me, and I handed her Mr. Quaff's card. Of course she remembered Mr. Quaff, he was such a wonderful person and a great actor. She asked me where I had met him and several other questions, and I knew right away that she was trying to get me to talk so that she could get a sample of my affliction.

The sample I gave her was a fair one.

She went on talking and asking me questions. And she acted as though she were considering my problem very seriously. But I had the impression that she felt I would be a nuisance and an encumbrance to the whole company.

I was wrong, though. Because, instead of making excuses and sending me on my way, she took me aside, and we sat down together. We had a long talk, and among the things she asked me was whether I had ever done anything to help cure myself of stammering.

"Oh, yes," I said. I told her how a long time ago I had read that Demosthenes, in ancient Greece, had taught himself to speak clearly by practicing with pebbles in his mouth. And I had done the same in our backyard, only, not having pebbles, I used marbles. And I told her that, even though I had done this faithfully for a long time, it didn't seem to help at all.

She listened to everything I told her. She was very patient. Then she said: "Come along. I don't know exactly what I have for you to do. But you come and join our group. I'll soon find a part for you—a good part, something really important."

The words "something really important" pleased me very much. Yes, I wanted very much, stammer or no stammer to be something important.

In this way I joined the group, and in time Emma Sheridan gave me some small parts to read. There were days when I read them fairly well, but on other days no two words were spoken clearly. On damp and rainy days my stammer was at its worst. But I enjoyed it all just the same, and I had a lot of fun. We met twice a week after school, and on Saturdays we had a long session.

One day Miss Sheridan announced that the group would

do a real play, a play in three acts, and that it would be presented with scenery and costumes in the auditorium. The tickets would cost ten cents, and the public would be invited. The play would be *The Prince and the Pauper*, a dramatization of Mark Twain's book. We were all delighted, and the very next time we met, Emma Sheridan gave out the parts. She stood in the middle of the room with a whole stack of typewritten booklets in her hand and all of us gathered around her.

"This one will be for you," she said, handing a small book to one of the girls. "And you should do well in this role," she said, handing a booklet to another. "And you, John, will play the Prince. And the Pauper—now let me see. These lines are just right for you," she said, giving another booklet to still another boy.

I stood by. I watched. I waited. Soon the last part was given out. And, just as I had feared, everyone was accounted for except me.

Then suddenly Miss Sheridan turned her head and, seeing me standing there very forlorn, said: "Oh!" She looked startled. "I was wondering where you were. I have a part for you. It's one of the most important parts of all. You're going to be the leader of the mob that saves the Prince from the ruffians. You are going to carry a cudgel."

My gloom lifted. I was happy. I smiled. Not only did I have a part, but I was going to carry a cudgel. I did not know what a cudgel was, but I assumed that it must be made of gold or silver and, like a scepter, give one authority. It was only later that I found out that a cudgel was only an Englishman's version of an Irish shillelagh.

I was very pleased to have a part, and I looked about to see if there were another play booklet that had been overlooked.

But Miss Sheridan said quickly: "No, there's no book. You must create this part yourself. There are no lines to be spoken. You do it all with gestures and grimaces. It's a part of feeling." Then she asked: "Can you growl?"

"Yes, I can growl," I answered.

"How many different ways can you growl?"

"Two or three."

"Oh," she said. "That won't do at all. We'll have to practice all kinds of growls. You see, when the Prince is threatened you will have to growl with disapproval and horror. When you gather your faithful mob together you'll use another type of growl. Then you will have an ugly growl for violence and a happy growl when the Prince is saved. You will have to study really hard, because you'll need about forty different growls, and they will have to be right. This is a very important part."

During the next four weeks I practiced growling. And I developed some growls that had never been heard before and have never been heard since.

The mob I led was gathered from the streets. At first we had only two or three in training. But as the rehearsals progressed we asked them to bring their brothers, cousins, and friends. In the end we had almost two dozen, and every one of them was smart. I trained them, and I know. They caught on to the growling right away, and they understood the signaling that I did with my cudgel. I was proud of this mob and of the unity with which they worked. Some of the other actors, even to the last day, forgot their lines or cues or other things, but this never happened with my mob. They were really good. And Miss Sheridan recognized what I had accomplished and said so in front of everybody.

At last the afternoon for the dress rehearsal arrived, and everything was in order. The scenery was in place and all the properties were on hand. We even had an iron seal borrowed from a Notary Public down the block. It was supposed to represent the Great Seal of England, which the young Prince used for cracking nuts. I was rather doubtful that the Great Seal of England looked like this, but since no one else said anything about it, I kept quiet.

Getting the stage all set for the dress rehearsal was fun. But the best part of all was when Miss Sheridan opened some big boxes and gave each one a costume. We put our costumes on, and then— Miss Sheridan opened a box filled to the top with wigs! She knew exactly which wig was intended for each of us. And I drew the biggest and wildest bright red wig ever constructed.

I put it on and looked in the mirror. What I saw frightened me. And since it frightened me so delightfully, I stamped about the room making fierce grimaces, growling and frightening all the others. With this red wig I was just uncontrollable.

The dress rehearsal went off very well. Of course a few people lagged in their timing and had to repeat their lines. But my mob was eager and quick, and only once or twice did we have to repeat an entrance or a growl.

However, Miss Sheridan had a lot of advice to give all

of us, and she made us repeat certain scenes. This she called "polishing the production." And she was right, because the production got better and better.

After a full afternoon of work the dress rehearsal was over and we were ready for the opening performance on the following Saturday afternoon. On this day the curtain would go up and we should appear before a real audience. We were ready.

The following Saturday, when all of us were in the dressing rooms putting on our costumes, and my mob and I were smudging up our faces with burnt cork to make them look dirty and ruffianlike, Mrs. Hirsh came in. The gold watch on her bosom was going up and down rapidly, for she was nervous and excited. "Now, nobody must miss his cues," she said. "We want this production to be really good, because we expect some distinguished visitors this afternoon."

That's all she said. And then she walked out.

A little later I noticed some of our group gathered around a peephole in the curtain. They were taking turns looking out at the audience. "There he is! He just came in with a lady," said the girl who was peering through the hole.

"Who? Who just came in?" I asked.

"Why, Mr. Mark Twain, the author."

"Mark Twain? Let me look. Which one is he?"

"He's in the fifth row. He has white hair and he's wearing a white suit."

"But it's winter," I said. "No one wears a white suit in winter."

"Mr. Mark Twain does," said the girl.

I thought it very strange for anyone to wear a white suit in wintertime. I pressed my eye to the peephole, and in the audience I did see a man with a great shock of white hair, dressed in a white suit.

Very soon the news was whispered about that the author of *The Prince and the Pauper, Tom Sawyer,* and *Huck Finn* was in the audience. Mrs. Hirsh had invited him, and he did not even have to pay for the tickets, because he was so famous.

I had read *Tom Sawyer, Huck Finn,* and also *Life on the Mississippi,* and somehow, even though with my own eyes I had seen Mark Twain sitting out there in the audience, I couldn't quite believe it was true. I had read a lot of books and seen a lot of books, but somehow or other I never believed that authors really existed. In my mind they were some kind of distant creatures, not really mortal.

I took another look through the peephole to make sure that Mark Twain was really outside. He was.

I went back to my mob. "Today, fellows," I said, "you've got to be good." I threatened them with my cudgel, and they could see that there was nothing make-believe in my gesture. But I didn't tell them the reason why.

At last there was a hush in the auditorium, the lights were dimmed, and the curtain went up. Miss Sheridan sat on a high stool in the wings and held the script ready to prompt anybody who forgot his lines. But no lines were forgotten, and as she quietly turned the pages she smiled. We could tell by her smile that everything was all right.

And since everything was going so well, we, the mob, were determined to do our part better than we had ever done it before. We rushed upon the stage with such menacing growls that we struck terror into the hearts of all. We could see the frightened faces of some of the children in the first rows, and the more frightened they looked, the more we were encouraged. We laid it on good and thick.

The whole play was a great success, and when the final curtain came down with a bang there was a lot of applause, with endless curtain calls. On the third curtain call I marched across the stage with my mob following in single file. We had smiles on our smudged faces, and we got a good loud hand for the work we had done.

When the curtain calls were over all piled downstairs into the dressing rooms. We took off our wigs and were just about to put our hands into the cold cream pot to remove our make-up, when Mrs. Hirsh appeared in the doorway. "Hurry! Hurry!" she said. "Come back on stage, all of you. Put on your wigs and bring your programs. Mr. Mark Twain is going to autograph them for you."

I put my big red wig back on, grabbed my program, and started for the door. Then I ran back and got my cudgel, my badge of office, so that Mark Twain would be sure to know which ruffian I was.

When I reached the stage some of the boys and girls were already in line, and Mark Twain was signing their programs. As I awaited my turn in line and came closer and closer, I watched Mark Twain every minute. He had happy eyes and deep crow's feet. His shock of white hair was very nice, but his white mustache worried me: it was badly stained by tobacco.

At last my turn came. He took my program, stepped back

a little, squinted his eyes, and looking at me said: "My, you were terrifying! You frightened the life out of me."

Then he laughed and signed his name in the margin of my program. But he didn't give it back to me right away. He seemed to be waiting for me to say something. But I kept my lips sealed, I wasn't going to let Mark Twain know that I stammered.

There was an awkward moment, and then he ran his fingers through my red wig. "You were all right," he said. Then he laughed again and shook my hand.

And when he laughed I laughed too.

As I walked away I thought that he was the nicest man in the whole world and that he had a perfect right to wear a white suit even in wintertime. He was a very special person.

Between running and the theater I had a very full after-school schedule, but I found time for one other interest, and that was music.

When I was younger I liked band music, later I liked organ music, and now that I was older I liked the piano. I had been taking lessons for a number of years, and I had lost my heart to the sound of the piano. I practiced willingly with a metronome, and I made fair progress. And I hoped some day to gain facility and be able to play wonderful pieces like my teacher. I often asked her when my lesson was over if she would please play something for me. And she was very nice and always did. I would sit and listen intently.

My teacher was one of the few persons I heard play, for she was the only one I knew who was an accomplished pianist. I knew several boys who, like me, were taking lessons, but they stammered on the piano as I did in speaking.

Occasionally, very infrequently, my mother would take me to a real concert. But since tickets for these concerts were rather expensive I went but rarely. However, I did once hear Paderewski, and I heard the great Chopin artist, De Pachmann. And any number of times I heard the famous Rafael Joseffy, who had been a pupil and secretary of Franz Liszt. But I didn't hear him in a concert hall. I heard him somewhere else.

One day after school, as I was walking along Fourteenth Street, I stopped to look at some pianos in the show window of Steinway Hall. And while I was standing there I heard, through an open window above, someone playing the piano. I listened. It was hauntingly beautiful, and I could not go away. But the maddening street noises interrupted the music.

I knew that the floors above the showroom in the Steinway Building were used as studios, and I thought that perhaps it wouldn't be wrong to go up into the hall and stand there quietly and listen. I should be able to hear much better, and I shouldn't disturb anybody. Of course, if the janitor or someone told me to get out, I would go right away. Deep inside I felt that it wasn't really right for me to go upstairs. But I wanted so badly to listen to the music that I finally climbed the broad flight of wooden stairs, flanked by a great mahogany balustrade each rung of which was carved like a piano leg. Then I walked softly down the broad dusty hall past several doors until I came to the one behind which someone was playing the piano. I stepped back a bit and stood on the opposite side of the hall, facing the door, next to some fire pails. I listened.

The music and the playing were beautiful—as beautiful as anything I had ever heard. Yet it was all spoiled for me because I feared that the janitor might arrive at any moment and send me off. And I also felt guilty because I was eavesdropping. This was a wrong thing to do, even when one was listening only to music. But I couldn't go. I stayed there in the hall.

Now and then the pianist would stop. Sometimes he played a piece all through, and sometimes he played only sections. Occasionally there was a long silence. Then he would begin again.

During one of these silences, as I waited for the playing to start again, the door suddenly opened, and there stood the pianist before me. There we were, facing each other. I was startled, and so was he. He just stood in the doorway with a large brass key in his hand and looked at me. I wanted to escape. I wanted to run away. But I couldn't. I had to say something. It was up to me to explain. But he spoke first, very gently.

"Are you looking for me—Rafael Joseffy?" he asked, speaking with a strong Hungarian accent.

I shook my head and swallowed hard. "No, sir," I said.

"Then you want something?"

"No, sir. I was only listening. I'm sorry." My face was burning, and he could certainly see the color of my embarrassment.

"You were just listening?" he said. He was not angry. And I knew immediately that he did not consider what I had done a crime. "You were listening," he repeated, "and I playing so badly!"

Now *he* seemed embarrassed. We just stood there.

Finally he spoke again. "You like the piano?"

"Very much, sir. Very much."

"All right. You wait here. I'll come right back."

He went down to the end of the hall and with his big brass key unlocked a door marked "Washroom." He was soon back, and he asked me to come into his studio.

"I am ashamed I was playing so badly. Without an audience I get careless. I will play the whole thing over for you. Sit down."

Two concert grand pianos stood side by side at one end of his large studio. The keyboards of both pianos were in line. They gave the impression of one long keyboard. Near by were several large bookcases filled with a library of music. I had never seen so many volumes before. And the wall opposite the bookcases was covered with autographed photographs and musical mementos. Joseffy sat at one of the pianos.

"What you heard outside was nothing but musical pish-pash. Now you will really hear something." He began to play.

As he played he sometimes closed his eyes and leaned his head far back, and at other times he bent over with his ear close to the keyboard as if trying to catch the inner quality of the tone. He was so completely absorbed in his playing that I know he forgot that there was someone sitting in the room. I sat very still and listened. And as I listened I watched him.

He had a big head and a shock of steel-gray hair. There was something pleasantly homely about his face, and there was a sadness about it too. And he had big hands with long fingers that moved freely and easily.

When he finished the composition he looked up and said, "It is one of the legends, 'St. Francis Preaching to the Birds.' Now I will play the other, 'St Francis Walking on the Waves.' "

I had never heard either of these pieces before, and it was not until later, when I asked my teacher, that I learned that they had been written by Franz Liszt. My teacher also told me that Joseffy had edited all of Liszt's works for G. Schirmer. But on this afternoon I only sat and listened, and it didn't matter to me that I didn't know the names of the pieces or who had composed them. I thought the St. Francis legends both very beautiful, and I recognized how difficult they were to play.

That afternoon Joseffy played several other pieces, and he stopped only when the door opened and a lady came in. She was carrying a leather music case and had come for her lesson. While they were talking together I got up and started slowly and quietly for the door. I was just stepping into the hall when Joseffy called after me: "Hey, you! Where are you going? Come back tomorrow."

"I can't come tomorrow, sir, I'm running."

He looked puzzled. "Where are you running to?"

"I'm a track runner on my school team."

"Oh, that kind of running." And he laughed. "Then come back the next day."

"Yes, sir, I will. Same time?"

"Yes, same time."

I went quickly, and as I was closing the door behind me I heard him say to the lady: "What good will running ever do him? It would be better if he listened to music."

Many times after that I went to Joseffy's studio and listened to him play. He always seemed to be happy to have an audience, and I was always happy to be there.

As I listened to him play, it seemed as though a whole new world opened before me. Before this, music had meant for me a pleasing tune, something that I could take home and whistle. It had been a kind of discourse in sound that posed a question in one phrase and answered it in the next. But now, alone with the great Joseffy in the intimacy of his studio, music became something different and wonderful. It surrounded me and made me a prisoner of its mood. And no one was ever a more willing captive. The voice of the music called to me, and I responded.

The music that he played seemed to me to be a great architecture of sound, an architecture that was in motion. And as the sound unfolded in my mind I saw great cliffs and ravines, walls of deep forests, and hidden mansions with towers and endless halls. Here in this land one could find all one's desires. And in all the visions that the music evoked for me there was a deep shadow in which I found hidden a sadness, a supreme sadness. It was in the envelopment of this shadow that the wonder of the visions came to be revealed.

Sometimes when Joseffy rested he would talk to me. He would ask me all kinds of questions about the music I had just heard, and I would try to tell him what I felt and what

I thought. And what I had to say, I am sure, must have sounded very trivial and foolish to his ears. But he listened patiently.

One day he was curious to know how I had first become interested in music, and I told him how, when I was young, I had gone to the park and listened to the bands. I said that this music had satisfied me until one day, passing a church not far from my home, I had heard the sound of a great organ. I had stopped and listened, and from that time on I no longer cared for band music. I went back to the church many times and stood on the sidewalk leaning against the railing. The resonance of the music filled me completely. I could even feel the vibrations of the low notes through the soles of my feet and through my hands as I held the railing. But in time organ music wearied me. I found the color of the music monotonous and drab, and I sought something different. It was then that I started taking piano lessons; and I found in the piano what I liked. It was colorful and capable of evoking a great variety of moods.

He listened to everything I said. He nodded his head. "The piano is a new instrument," he said. "It developed slowly from the spinet, harpsichord, and clavichord. Bach played the organ and clavichord. And even Chopin did not have a piano as we know it today—a full, rich instrument."

I had many visits alone with Joseffy, but there were also times when others came into the studio—people whose names I do not know. Many were concert artists and came to play over their programs for him before appearing in public. I was too ignorant to recognize who they were, and I was afraid to ask, but I know that some of them were the great pianists of the day.

I often wondered why Joseffy allowed me to come to his studio. His friends were all people of accomplishment, and I was nobody and knew so little!

And one day as I was leaving the studio with one of his younger pupils, I spoke of this mystery. The student answered: "Oh, it is easy to explain. Joseffy is shy. He is so painfully shy that he can never play in public. He is afraid to face an audience. He is shy, and you are shy. And so when he found you standing in the hall, he told me— Two frightened people facing each other! He understood immediately how you felt, for he had suffered so often from the same thing!"

During my last year in high school I wrote an essay on Abraham Lincoln. Ten short handwritten pages, and my future was settled. I spent only a few brief hours on this essay, but it dictated the course of the rest of my life.

The reason I had a few brief hours to spend on it was that I had recently given up running, acting, and visiting Joseffy's studio. I had given up running partly because of the remark I had overheard Joseffy make and partly because, no matter how fast I ran, there were others who ran faster. I had given up acting because there are so few parts that are written exclusively for growling; besides, theatrical training did not seem to be curing my stammer. My visits to Joseffy's studio had ended because he had left New York.

Thus it was that at the beginning of my fourth year in

high school I found myself at a loose end. Thus it was that I had spare time to write an essay.

Now this essay was not an ordinary classroom essay. It was written with a purpose. It was written to be entered in a contest run by the *New York Times* to celebrate the hundredth anniversary of the birth of Abraham Lincoln.

I was not too anxious to enter this contest, but my English teacher urged me into it. He thought I was just the right kind of boy to represent Stuyvesant High School in such a competition. He picked some other boys, too, but he seemed to have his beady eye on me.

I tried hard to argue my way out of this honor, but my teacher was insistent. He said it was easy. He said that all I had to do was to write a few pages telling exactly why I liked Abraham Lincoln. I did not have to worry about the word "essay," I did not have to worry about "history," I did not have to worry about "style." I had only to write what I felt.

I was not enthusiastic, but I knew that I should have to do as my teacher said. There was only one good thing about it all: I liked Abraham Lincoln. I thought he was the finest man that ever lived. So I got to work. And what I knew and felt about Lincoln just filled ten pages. These I brought to school, and my teacher sent them off to the *New York Times.*

I was glad when the essay was out of my hands and I could forget all about it. And I did forget all about it. I returned to the peaceful routine of my everyday life. And that is how I thought life was always going to be.

But suddenly, about a month later, my peace was broken. The *New York Times* announced that I had won a silver medal! At first I did not believe it. But my teacher showed me the letter announcing the award. It was true.

A few days later, at assembly, our principal called me to the stage. He read the letter from the *New York Times,* delivered a speech, and presented me with the medal. In his speech he said that I would certainly turn out to be an author. And he also said something about the fact that learning to use my hands in this manual training high school would be a great asset to me in my profession. Exactly how this would work he did not explain, but I believed what he said, because his words were so complimentary.

I think the presentation of this medal was one of the highlights of my life. It was a beautiful ceremony and a beautiful medal. On one side was a fine head of Abraham Lincoln encircled with the legend "With malice toward none, with charity for all." On the other side of the medal my name was engraved right under the inscription, "Awarded by the *New York Times.*"

That morning when assembly was over a crowd gathered around me, and my medal went from one hand to another. But I watched it carefully. And I was glad when I got it back and could put it safely in its box.

As soon as school was over that day I rushed home to Grandma and Grandpa. Of course, I had brought medals home before, but they were for athletics, and Grandma and Grandpa were not impressed with physical prowess. But this medal was different. It had been awarded for intellectual accomplishment. Of this they approved.

Grandpa immediately borrowed my medal. He said he wanted to show it to certain people when they came into the store. I didn't like him to do this. It was embarrassing. But there was no arguing with him. Besides, he said that the medal would be safer in his store than in my pocket. I didn't want to lose it, did I? He also said that he would be discreet; he would show it only to certain persons. I didn't like to doubt Grandpa's word, but I had a fear that this would not be so. And I was right.

Grandpa was so proud and so enthusiastic that, with every cigar and bag of snuff he sold, with every classified advertisement he accepted, out would come the medal. And each time he would deliver a little speech on how I had been chosen for this honor and how the principal had said that I would become a writer. And each time the speech would end with the same words: "The medal is made by Tiffany."

Everyone was much impressed with the fact that a Fifty-second Street boy had so distinguished himself. In a day or so I was the talk of the neighborhood. The firemen and policemen all smiled proudly when they saw me. Mr. Schultz shook my hand and congratulated me. Mr. Hadley said that Lincoln was one of the greatest of all Americans and he was glad that I should be interested in him. Mrs. O'Leary said: "I knew it all the time. Even when he was nothing but a little one, running around here, it was easy to see that he was bright as a button."

And Mr. Quaff said: "Writing is a very good profession. It is much like acting. One doesn't need expensive equipment like a Stradivarius fiddle, a Steinway grand, or medical instruments like doctors or dentists. All a writer needs is a ten-cent bottle of ink and a few sheets of paper, and he's in business! Besides, actors and writers don't have to spend

years studying in universities. Life is their university, their
academy humane. Every experience they have, good and bad,
every bit of knowledge they acquire, is material for their
profession. Life gives them freely what they need."

I liked what Mr. Quaff said, especially the part about
writers not having to go to universities. But I knew Grandpa
had made up his mind that I was going to go to college, and
my mother was backing him up. In fact, I was already enrolled at Yale. I was to begin there the following fall.
Nevertheless, I was hopeful that he might give in, and I
repeated a few of Mr. Quaff's words. But Grandpa was firm.

"I don't care what Mr. Quaff says about life being an
academy humane," he said. "You have to go to college first,
then you can write anything you want." Grandpa was angry.
"Do you think history, anthropology, and philosophy are
nothing at all? These things you won't find on the streets of
New York!"

I could see that I was up against a stone wall and that I
should be leaving for college in September. I dropped the
whole argument and went about the neighborhood enjoying
my fame.

But behind the glory and the sunshine there were dark
rumblings. Some said that they knew the *New York Times*
meant well, but they didn't think that young people should
be encouraged to become authors. To take up writing as a
profession could only lead to grief. They told all kinds of
gloomy stories of how some authors had written their mas-
terpieces in jail, how others had starved to death, and how
still others had become hopeless drunkards. All in all, to become an author was not a good thing.

I listened to all these harrowing tales, but somehow or other they didn't frighten me. Having grown up in a big city like New York and rubbed elbows with experience, I had no fear that life would ever prove so perplexing to me that I should land in jail, starve to death, or become a drunkard. I felt that I should find my way through life as I had always found my way through the streets of my enchanted island.

Here on Manhattan I had lived in a miniature world with people of all kinds and with a sampling of almost every situation and emotion that life could provide. The gloomy stories that I heard didn't frighten me. And I decided that I would be a writer anyway.

Besides, when I wrote those ten pages on Lincoln, I discovered a wonderful thing: I could say what I felt without talking. Had I attempted to speak the same words that I had written, I should have stammered so badly that no one would have had the patience to listen. But from now on, with pen and ink, I should be able to communicate. I should be able to tell everything I knew, everything I felt, everything I hoped.

Then, too, I believed that Mr. Quaff was right when he said that life provided a writer with the materials for his profession, that living day by day and mixing with all kinds of people provided an author with everything he needed. And I felt that, even though I was still young, I had a good start; I had already accumulated a lot of experiences. I had a whole bushelful!

I knew how to run a cigar store and a classified agency, I knew something about the newspaper world, shoemaking,

carpentry, farming, politics, labor, and music. I knew how to
paint a wooden Indian, how to brew a war between two Irish
saloons, how to judge a good horse, and how to wire an
electric bell. I even knew something about trust-busting.
Until now all these things had seemed unrelated and mean-
ingless. But now that I had decided to become a writer, like
the crazy pieces of a jigsaw puzzle they fitted together, and,
besides, they took on value. They were all things that I
might some day use.

This bushelful of experience was a valuable gift that life
had dumped right into my lap free of charge. And I realized
that as I lived on, growing older and older, if I remained
curious and interested in the world about me life would
continue giving freely. In time I should have a warehouse
full of events and a whole portrait gallery of people to draw
upon.

A bushelful of experience was a good start. And now that
I had decided to become a writer I looked forward to going
on from one experience and adventure to another. Now I
felt that my life had a direction. I felt that I was no longer
a boy. I felt that from now on I was grown up.